Slovenians *in* Cleveland

Slovenians *in* Cleveland

A HISTORY

ALAN F. DUTKA

THE
History
PRESS

Published by The History Press
Charleston, SC
www.historypress.net

Front cover, top: courtesy of Special Collections, Michael Schwartz Library, Cleveland State
University; *bottom*: courtesy of St. Clair Superior Development Corporation.
Back cover, top: courtesy of St. Clair Superior Development Corporation; *bottom*: courtesy of
Special Collections, Michael Schwartz Library, Cleveland State University.

First published 2017

Manufactured in the United States

ISBN 9781625859747

Library of Congress Control Number: 2017940954

Contents

CONTENTS

Foreword

Cleveland author Alan Dutka provides a glimpse into the lives of some of Cleveland Slovenians' most intriguing, inspiring and tragic stories. Dutka has been writing about hidden pieces of Cleveland history for over a decade, including his books on Cleveland's AsiaTown, Cleveland's Millionaires' Row, East Fourth Street, Short Vincent, downtown movie theaters and some of the darker days in the city's history in *Cleveland Calamities*.

Dutka, who grew up in the shadow of Cleveland's Industrial Valley and the factories and mills that employed many Slovenian immigrants, dives into the subject by exploring the lives and struggles of the area's first Slovenians in the late ninetieth century and follows several waves of immigrants through the twentieth century and into the present century. Like many immigrant groups, Slovenians survived and prospered by banding together to form and build their own churches, social halls and businesses, all of which were staples in the daily life of these ethnic enclaves. Cleveland is home to eight Slovenian national homes, venues that play a key role in the northeast Ohio community by hosting weddings, parties, concerts, political rallies and other social events.

Cleveland, home to the largest population of Slovenian people outside of Slovenia, has several historically Slovenian neighborhoods, including St. Clair, Collinwood and Newburgh. These close-knit communities provided generations of Slovenians with social networks, recreation, religion, education, arts and culture, as well as a unique culinary environment where traditional recipes and food have lived on through generations. The role these neighborhoods played in shaping the history of Cleveland cannot be understated.

Though many Slovenians have moved from the old neighborhoods into the suburbs and exurbs, the national homes are still considered important social hubs for the community. They continue to be anchors for these neighborhoods as residents put the pieces back together after the foreclosure crisis of 2008–12. An affinity for the history of these neighborhoods has captivated a younger generation and has given rise to a number of new events, including the annual Kurentovanje festival, held in the St. Clair neighborhood. It attracts thousands of people to the area to experience Slovenian culture.

In this book, Dutka provides entertaining information and stories that give a glimpse into what life was like for Cleveland's Slovenians in the last 135 years. Life wasn't always easy, and there have been plenty of challenges along the way. But with each challenge came an opportunity for accomplishment—as you will read, there have certainly been many accomplishments, and many more are yet to come.

—James Amendola
Industrial/Commercial Manager,
St. Clair Superior Development Corporation

Foreword

Growing up a third-generation Slovenian in Slavic Village (Newburgh), Cleveland, I have been hanging out at the Slovenian National Home ("the Nash") on East Eightieth Street my entire life. My grandfather is a past president of the organization, and his leadership in the Slavic Village community has been an inspiration such that my own neighborhood development company, Sonny Day, bears his nickname.

I became actively involved at the Nash in 2011 as director of development, with the goal of helping the aging yet resilient organization continue to enjoy its fraternal activities while revitalizing and preserving the use of its historic property. Since that time, I have had countless questions for my grandfather (who passed away in 2006) regarding the beautiful, one-hundred-year-old, hand-built social hall and the fraternal aspects of the organization, along with its relationship with the other, now-century-old Slovenian Homes throughout Cleveland. Truly, if walls could talk....

In this book, Alan Dutka answers many of the questions I've had over the years (except "Why is the hall painted so pink?" and "Why are there so many pairs of size nines in the Lanes?"), and he paints a comprehensive picture of the Slovenian culture from a palette filled by way of exploring his own, genuine curiosity. I've had the pleasure to spend some time with the author, sharing only my point of view; his genuine nature rings true here in print, recalling conversations and interviews throughout the Cleveland Slovenian community.

It's remarkable to ponder how these immigrants were able to build these National Homes a century ago, especially with the backdrop of the economic and other challenges highlighted in this book. It's even more remarkable to consider these Slovenes as only one of the many immigrant groups pursuing a similar happiness in America and building this diverse city of Cleveland despite facing similar challenges.

The bonds made—galvanized by the wars, the Great Depression and beyond—have been celebrated for generations in these social halls. It's part of the rich history that one cannot describe but can only feel when standing inside the magnificent structures. Dutka provides the context for the importance of preserving this existing fabric and honoring the past as we plan for the future.

For me, many of the recalled names, places and events ring a bell. Whether or not they do for the reader, the spirit of fraternity, tenacity and love is something we can all relate to. It's a charming grit.

Na Zdravje!

—Anthony J. Trzaska
Director of Development, Slovenian National Home (Newburgh)
Founder, Sonny Day Development Corporation

Preface

Although I have an abundance of ethnic blood flowing though my veins, I doubt if a DNA test would reveal any consequential Slovenian heritage. Nonetheless, I consider myself sort of an honorary Slovenian. I attended the same high school as students whose Slovenian parents had remained in Cleveland's very first Slovenian enclave. By the time I had become a teenager, rock 'n' roll had generally relegated polka music to a non-hip status, enjoyed only by old people in their thirties or older. But in the neighborhood where I grew up, teenagers still enthusiastically purchased the latest Frankie Yankovic polka albums at the Fleet Avenue record store.

Furthermore, for the past forty years, I have been married to a 100 percent Slovenian woman. Eating my mother-in-law's potica and krofe became enjoyable experiences, and even listening to my father-in-law's Sunday afternoon selection of radio stations playing Cleveland-style polkas had its redeeming moments. Therefore, although I knew I had a lot of learning ahead of me, I felt comfortable researching and writing a story about Cleveland's Slovenians. And I received an amazing amount of assistance within the Slovenian communities. A priest opened his rectory door, and a butcher unlocked his smokehouse. Residents supplied pictures, and a historian warned me of potential problems in interpreting past events.

Through seven generations, Cleveland Slovenians have contributed greatly to the city's political advancement, musical heritage, food scene and sports legacy. Early immigrants toiled in steel mills and factories; some later became successful entrepreneurs. Their children and grandchildren, along with new generations of refugees, contributed to healthcare advances and provided legal expertise. The rich history also contains tales of political turmoil, social upheaval, infighting and unimaginable tragedy. I hope you enjoy my attempt to retell the 140-year history of Cleveland's Slovenians.

Acknowledgements

I would like to thank the following people and institutions: At Azman's Market, Frank Azman; at the Cleveland Public Library, Stacy Brisker (Special Collections), Kelly Ross Brown (Special Collections), Bill Chase (Special Collections), Nicholas Durda (Photographs), Thomas Edwards (Map Collection), Pamela J. Eyerdam (Fine Arts), Olivia Hoge (History), Adam Jaenke (Photographs), Brian Meggitt (Photographs) and Ann Marie Wieland (Archives). At Cleveland State University, I wish to thank William C. Barrow (Special Collections) and Lynn M. Duchez Bycko (Special Collections), as well as John Rodrigue and Rick Delaney at The History Press. Thanks go out to James Amendola and Michael Fleming at the St. Clair Superior Development Corporation. At St. Mary of the Assumption Catholic Church, I would like to thank Reverend John Kumse and Jo Ann Kosoglov Stinziano; at St. Vitus Catholic Church, I wish to acknowledge Stan J. Kuhar. Anthony J. Trzaska at Sonny Day Development Corporation was very helpful. And, finally, I would like to thank the following individuals: Frances "Tanny" Babic, Nick Babic, Frank Bokar, Mary Louise Daley, Priscilla Dutka, Diane Ghorbanzadeh, Anthony W. Hiti, Amy Pease, Al Perko, Elaine Peskar, Tony Peskar, Beth Piwkowski, Susan Millavec-Schumacher, Frank Strainer and Bob Zabak.

Introduction

Cleveland's first Slovenians emigrated from a mostly mountainous agrarian region in Austria, about the size of Massachusetts, extending from the Julian Alps southward along the Dalmatian Coast. Unfavorable inheritance laws, landownership regulations and infertile soil prevented many peasants from rising above their state of prolonged poverty, in which farmers and their sons sometimes shared the same pair of shoes.

Many of these laborers and small farmers journeyed to Cleveland to accumulate the money needed to return to their homeland and purchase homes, productive farmland or even chicken farms, which did not require exceptionally good soil. Most Slovenian immigrant men, traveling without their families, expected to return to Austria within a few years.

Enduring two weeks of cramped and unhealthy living quarters in the bowels of ocean vessels, these immigrants paid twenty dollars to travel across the Atlantic Ocean to New York City. Most carried a picture of the family they had left behind, enough money to pay immigration fees and a Bible to provide inspiration. They hoped their wages would prevent them from becoming hungry while allowing them to send a portion of their earnings back to the wives and children who remained in Austria.

Railroads transported the immigrants from New York to Cleveland, where they would work as laborers in factories. In 1892, an unskilled Cleveland steelworker earned fourteen cents an hour; fifteen years later, hourly wages had increased only to sixteen cents. But a laborer working six twelve-hour days earned in one day what a peasant worker in Slovenia

Many Slovenians immigrating to Cleveland planned to return to the agricultural regions surrounding Ljubljana, Slovenia's principal city, shown here in 1934. *Courtesy of Cleveland Public Library, Photograph Collection.*

received in a week for toiling seventeen-hour days beginning at 4:00 a.m. and continuing until 9:00 p.m.

The cost of rentals in Cleveland boarding homes ranged from five to seven dollars per month and often included amenities such as meals and laundry service. The tenants' shift work and long hours allowed landlords to double up occupancies—two laborers would share a room. Although this situation was not always convenient, Slovenian peasants had already learned in their homeland to cope with dwellings consisting of a single room and having to share kitchens and bathrooms with other residents.

Hardworking and frugal Slovenians needed between three and five years to save enough money to start afresh in Austria. Although many Slovenians did return to their homeland, a significant number made Cleveland their permanent home; others completed multiple trips across the ocean between Slovenia and Cleveland. Employment prospects in Cleveland, along with opportunities to launch businesses, greatly exceeded those available in Austria. America's political stability also far exceeded that of Europe where Austrian Slovenians dealt with multiethnic discords within their own empire along with conflicts with Russia and the Ottoman Empire. Beginning in the 1880s, major Slovenian settlements within Cleveland developed in southeast Newburgh, along St. Clair Avenue and in Collinwood. Through the decades, smaller Slovenian communities also arose in the city's West Park and Denison Avenue neighborhoods.

Well before the start of World War I, a "Slavic awakening" had divided Slovenians in Austria into two distinct groups: a right-wing segment, loosely aligned with the Catholic Church and desiring to remain under the Austrian umbrella, and a left-wing faction favoring separation from Austria. This political division intensified and persisted for decades, manifesting itself in Cleveland's Slovenian settlements and continuing through generations. As just one example, the Collinwood neighborhood still maintains two Slovenian meeting places, an original right-wing Slovenian National Home on Holmes Avenue and a one-time left-leaning Slovenian Workman's Home on Waterloo Road.

Immigration lessened when the perils of World War I hindered travel across the Atlantic Ocean. After the war, neighboring Italy, Austria and Hungary all controlled portions of the former Slovenian community; each subjected Slovenians to varying degrees of ethnic and cultural assimilation. Italy, ruling about one-quarter of the Slovenians' prewar territory, banned the use of the Slovenian language, modified surnames to reflect Italian translations and abolished Slovenian cultural societies and customs.

In 1941, residents of picturesque Ljubljana endured the turmoil of World War II. *Courtesy of Cleveland Public Library, Photograph Collection.*

Immigration to Cleveland increased again as many Slovenians chose to abandon their homeland rather than being subjected to absorption by other countries.

The remaining Austrian Slovenians joined with neighboring regions to shape the Kingdom of the Serbs, Croats and Slovenes, a region renamed Yugoslavia in 1929. In the 1920s, stricter U.S. laws limited legal immigration. Yet Slovenians continued their migration to Cleveland by first immigrating to Canada and then crossing the largely unsupervised border into the United States. By 1923, Cleveland's population of forty thousand Slovenians exceeded that of every city in the world except for the sixty-eight thousand living in Ljubljana, Slovenia's principal city.

In Cleveland, following World War II, right- and left-wing Slovenians factions staged separate parades, one week apart, down St. Clair Avenue. At the time, the city supported two daily local Slovenian newspapers, one conservative and the other liberal.

In the late 1940s and early 1950s, many political refugees immigrated to Cleveland. Established Slovenians frequently viewed these newcomers (often incorrectly) as either German collaborators or communist sympathizers. Mainstream newspaper articles depicted the refugees as professionals (doctors, lawyers and professors) and often contrasted them with earlier immigrants, described as uneducated factory workers. These characterizations created more division among Slovenians. In the 1960s and '70s, Slovenians' interest in Cleveland increased as Yugoslavia relaxed its restrictions on immigrating to the United States.

Slovenians later migrated to the suburbs of Euclid, Maple Heights, Garfield Heights, Eastlake, Willoughby and Painesville; some joined an established settlement in nearby Lorain. In 1986, about ninety thousand people of Slovenian ancestry resided in Greater Cleveland, third only to Ljubljana and Maribor (both cities in the Slovenian portion of Yugoslavia).

In the early 1990s, the Slovenian segment of Yugoslavia withdrew to form the new nation of Slovenia. Thus, prior to 1992, incoming Slovenians emigrated not from an actual country called Slovenia but, rather, from an ethnic territory of Slovenian-speaking people in Austria, part of the region later named Yugoslavia.

1

Newburgh

The Lure of the Steel Mills

John Pintar, the first known Slovenian visitor to Cleveland, arrived in 1879 but returned to his homeland after a stay of only five months. Four years later, he revisited the United States and soon migrated back to Cleveland. Unable to find suitable employment, he walked westward and, after thirty-three days, ended up in a Slovenian section of Pueblo, Colorado. With the prospects for finding work no better in the West, Pintar walked fourteen-hundred miles back to Cleveland, where he remained until his death more than three decades later.

In October 1881, Slovenian immigrant Joseph Turk survived an unusually long and arduous twenty-eight-day trip across the Atlantic Ocean. Speaking little English, Turk stepped off a train in Cleveland with no friends or relatives to assist him. He secured lodgings on Marble Avenue and found a job in a nearby shop that paid $1 for a ten-hour workday. By the end of one year, he had sent $100 back to his family in Slovenia.

Within two years, Turk had built a home on Marble Avenue, near the Newburgh steel mills where he now worked, and opened a prosperous saloon to serve as a meeting place for the thirty or so other Slovenians who had settled in the neighborhood. His daughter Gertrude joined him in 1885, becoming Cleveland's first female Slovenian immigrant. By 1892, Turk had acquired a grocery store and three boarding homes. He presented the saloon to his daughter as a wedding gift and procured two more drinking establishments as presents for his sons.

In the late nineteenth century, the Newburgh Steel Mill provided employment for unskilled Slovenian immigrants. *Courtesy of Cleveland Public Library, Photograph Collection.*

Overly generous to newly arriving Slovenian immigrants, Turk lost his financial resources in an 1893 business downturn. For a time, he relied on the earnings of his two teenage sons. He eventually purchased land in Euclid, Ohio, where he grew grapes for making wine. He opened yet another saloon, this time in the Collinwood neighborhood.

John Bradac, who immigrated to Cleveland in 1890 at the age of twenty-two, resided in the Newburgh neighborhood for fifty-seven years. He opened saloons on Burke and Marble Avenues (about a block from each other) and aided more than eight hundred Slovenians in obtaining U.S. citizenship. Frank Kuznik arrived in Cleveland in 1900 and worked in the steel mills for five years before purchasing a tavern on East Eighty-First Street and a home above the tavern.

These and other saloons served as refuges where Slovenian immigrants, most unfamiliar with the English language and American customs, could share comradeship, debate politics, sing songs, play card games, participate in neighborhood gatherings and even obtain employment from factory foremen, who often recruited employees at the various saloons.

Drinking establishments enabled entrepreneurial Slovenians a straightforward entry into the business world if they agreed to sell beer manufactured by only one brewery. In exchange for this exclusive arrangement, the brewer provided essential expertise in composing property rental agreements, obtaining liquor licenses, securing bank financing and assisting in the training and paperwork required to acquire U.S. citizenship. With a multitude of brewers located in Cleveland, Slovenians experienced little difficulty in obtaining an obliging sponsor.

For Slovenian immigrants not interested in the business world, steady employment could be found in nearby factories, such as the American Steel and Wire Company, the Cleveland Rolling Mills and the Emma Furnace plant. John Horvath, settling in Cleveland in 1890, worked for American Steel and Wire for forty-one years. The plant employed Anton Gliha from 1900 to 1941 and Andrew Slack for decades following his 1898 arrival. Gliha died in his Aetna Road home above his own business, the Kozy Korner Tavern. Frank Strazar, the oldest of fourteen children, came to Cleveland in 1912 at the age of nineteen. After leaving his family's Slovenian farm, he secured employment at the steel plant. Catering to immigrants' love of music, the steel mill even organized a company band that presented concerts throughout the city.

With the advent of the automobile, the General Electric Company, located in the Hough neighborhood, also employed many Newburgh Slovenians. Eight to ten people would squeeze into an automobile to commute from the Broadway neighborhood. Immigrant John Strekal mastered the meat-cutting business as an employee of Swift and Company. Later, he and his wife, Mary, operated a grocery store and meat market for thirty years on East Eightieth Street. Mary lived her entire life above the store, as did her daughter, Mrs. Victor Matjasic.

Agnes Zagar, born on East 80th Street, moved one block east to make way for construction of the Slovenian National Home. During World War II, she worked at the Ohio Crankshaft Company on Harvard Avenue. Later employed by the Gottfried Clothing Company (located on Broadway Avenue at East 131st Street), she became a union steward and later chairman of the International Garment Workers Union. She served as a director of the Slovenian National Home for twenty-five years until she reached the age of eighty-five, four years prior to her death.

The approximate boundaries of this small Slovenian enclave were Union Avenue (north), Aetna Road (south), East Seventy-Eighth Street (west) and East Eighty-Second Street (east). Once farmland owned by Lorenzo Carter

(Cleveland's first settler) and his descendants, the Carter family sold the land for subdivision in the 1870s. Construction of homes began a decade later. To the west, Polish and Czech groups settled the neighborhoods between East Seventy-Eighth Street and Broadway Avenue. To the east, about ten sets of railroad tracks isolated East Eighty-Second Street from East Eighty-Eighth Street, the latter becoming part of a different neighborhood. The westernmost railroad track almost abutted the backs of the homes on East Eighty-Second Street. The tight fit allowed residents in their backyards to physically shake hands with the engineer of a passing train.

In the 1930s and '40s, the close-knit community enjoyed summer picnics. At least one accordion player provided the accompaniment as picnickers sang old Slovenian songs and played baseball. Members of a teenage group made their own costumes for annual plays (mostly consisting of songs and jokes) staged at the local Slovenian Home. During the Depression, boarders occupied beds in most of the rooms of the houses except for the kitchen.

Along with neighborhood churches, Slovenian settlements constructed halls, usually called Slovenian National Homes. Functioning as meeting places and entertainment venues, these halls hosted local gatherings, political assemblies, boxing and wrestling matches, cultural programs and Friday evening fish fries. On October 19, 1919, the Newburgh neighborhood celebrated the laying of the cornerstone for the Newburgh Slovenian National Home, to be located on East Eightieth Street. The home opened the following June and, in 1949, expanded by adding still-existing bowling alleys and a large ballroom built to accommodate seven hundred persons.

The National Home is still in operation. Today, the basement area under the original meeting room is a barroom featuring a working jukebox and a non-operational wooden telephone booth. No ladies' room exists in this part of the hall, since females were not allowed to enter the barroom when the facility first opened. Today, the National Home is a venue for weddings, comedy shows, fish fries, clambakes, Browns and Cavaliers watch parties and even a performance by members of the Cleveland Orchestra.

On the other side of the railroad tracks, the Slovenian Labor Auditorium on Prince Avenue also staged cultural events and wedding receptions and served as a public meeting place. The Socialist Party of America used the auditorium for its 1922 national convention. In the 1930s, the facility hosted meetings of the Russian Democratic Club. In 1932, three pistol shots interrupted the music of an accordion band entertaining at a Slovenian society dance. Twenty-one-year-old Carl Napoli had confronted Joseph Kravas (age forty-four) regarding Joseph's advances toward the mother of

Carl's eighteen-year-old wife. As a fistfight continued, Carl, believing Joseph had pulled a knife, shot Joseph three times, once in the hip and twice in the arm. Extensively remodeled in 1949, the labor auditorium is now the home of the New Galilee Baptist Church.

The neighborhood supported grocery stores, meat markets, a barbershop and a tailor shop. Trucks containing milk, ice, produce, baked goods, fish and waffles made periodic visits to the community. A grandmother, who spoke no English and never left the neighborhood, explained to her grandchildren that she had everything she needed right in the community—her church, a grocery store, a butcher shop and a funeral home.

Three generations of the Perko family lived above their grocery store, which incorporated a smokehouse in the backyard. During the Depression, the family offered credit, sometimes extending for years, to struggling neighbors. In the 1950s, an A&P supermarket debuted on Broadway Avenue, but it acquired little business from Slovenians, who remained loyal to the Perko family, who had helped them survive the Depression.

Mathew Sirk's store on East Eighty-Second Street, later owned by Frank Sirk, offered an amazing array of merchandise, including penny candy, ice cream, beer and liquor. It also had one solitary bowling alley.

After his barbershop closed for the day, Anthony (Bill) Strainer traveled to the homes of executives to supply evening haircuts for managers who had little time during working hours. Beginning in the 1920s and until the mid-1960s, Strainer operated his shop on East Eightieth Street. The site is now a parking lot for the Newburgh Slovenian Home.

Following World War II, Edward J. Zabak and his brothers organized a polka band. For more than forty-three years, Edward also owned Zabak's Tavern, located on Union Avenue at East Seventy-Eighth Street. The tavern's small stage sometimes accommodated multiple bands participating in impromptu polka jam sessions. Patrons desiring to dance maneuvered around a tiny dance floor, artfully learning how to step around each other without creating a crash. Zabak's children, sleeping in a bedroom directly above the dance floor, closed their eyes nearly every night listening to polka music seeping up through the floor.

From the 1920s into the 1960s, adventurous Newburgh residents traveled north down Broadway Avenue to partake in additional shopping, grocery and banking alternatives. Some residents walked as far as East Fifty-Fifth Street, whose intersection with Broadway Avenue comprised a thriving retail district. At times, these jaunts included a visit to one of four movie theaters along the route—the Market Square, Grand, New

Broadway and Olympia. To the east, the Union and Union Square movie houses presented even more options.

A few creative neighborhood teenage boys developed their own forms of entertainment. One of the more unusual escapades involved the use of railroad "dynamite caps." Railroad companies placed these two-inch-square caps on tracks to warn engineers that another train had stopped in an unexpected place. The loud noise created by a cap would alert the engineer to slow down and exercise extreme caution. Raiding a parked caboose used to store the caps, the Slovenian urchins would steal the noisemakers and place them on Broadway Avenue streetcar tracks. In addition to creating an earsplitting clamor, the caps at times knocked the streetcars right off their tracks. Another imaginative prank involved filling old, unwanted purses with human feces. The boys would throw the purses on Broadway Avenue and enjoy the surprise when a passerby retrieved the purse by placing his hand in it.

Counterbalancing the mischievous boys, a few Slovenian girls mastered the art of creating exquisite bobbin lace, a tradition learned at an early age in Slovenia. The artistic work at times produced family heirlooms, such clothing used at baptismal and confirmation ceremonies and as decorations on a ring bearer's pillow. The lace also beautified folk costumes and liturgical dress.

In the early 1970s, the Newburgh neighborhood exhibited its first outward signs of decline—the closing of the St. Lawrence Church School. The Slovenian presence markedly deteriorated in the ensuing decades. Today, the still-open National Home and the former St. Lawrence Church are among the few visible reminders of Cleveland's first Slovenian neighborhood.

2

St. Lawrence Church

Newburgh's Slovenian Foundation

Most Newburgh Slovenians initially celebrated mass in the basement of the nearby Holy Name Catholic Church (located on Broadway Avenue near Harvard Avenue), but the immigrants never felt comfortable in the predominately Irish church. A few, yearning to worship in an established Slovenian church, endured a reasonably long jaunt to St. Vitus near St. Clair Avenue. Finally, on May 11, 1902, more than three thousand mostly Slovenian individuals celebrated the cornerstone-laying ceremony for St. Lawrence Catholic Church and its affiliated school, both to be located on East Eightieth Street in the heart of Newburgh's Slovenian community. Three bands provided the musical entertainment for the joyful occasion. Bishop Jacob Trobec of St. Cloud, Minnesota (America's only Slovenian bishop at the time), delivered the principal speech. The new church began with about eight hundred members.

The quickly built, two-story, brick Romanesque building combined a school on one floor and a place of worship on the other. Reverend Francis Kerze, the church's first priest, had previously been an assistant pastor at St. Vitus Church. Along with delivering spiritual messages, Kerze dealt with numerous issues involving both the church's parishioners and the community. In 1905, when Cleveland examined the impact of railroad train smoke, the city appointed Kerze as a special deputy inspector to report, on a daily basis, the conditions around the church, school and neighborhood.

On several occasions, when ill feelings arose between differing factions of the church, malcontents stoned Kerze's home. One evening, an unusually unruly crowd broke a window in the rectory. The priest pulled out a revolver and fired a shot, allegedly to frighten the rowdies away. Police arrested Kerze on a charge of shooting with intent to wound, but the case was quickly dismissed. Following Kerze's seven-year tenure at St. Lawrence, Reverend Joseph Lavric served as pastor until 1915. The next priest led the church for forty-seven years.

In the 1870s, Simon Oman emigrated from Slovenia to Brockway Township, Minnesota, one of North America's oldest Slovenian settlements. On May 22, 1879, Simon and his wife welcomed John J. Oman into the world, the second of their eleven children. John gave up school in the fifth grade to work on his parents' farm. After later toiling as a water boy at a locomotive plant and as a lumberjack, fireman and miner, he entered a Minnesota seminary.

In 1912, a year after his ordainment, Reverend Oman reluctantly departed the picturesque Brockway setting for an assignment at Cleveland's St. Vitus Church. Three years later, the young, American-born priest, who lacked a good command of the Slovenian language, became head pastor at St. Lawrence. Any initial misgivings on the parishioners' part seemed to quickly evaporate. Oman taught the congregation enough English for them to pass citizenship examinations and stressed teaching the Slovenian language in the church school. Following his 1962 retirement, Oman returned to Brockway. When he died four years later, his funeral mass took place in the same church where he had been baptized.

Between 1910 and 1920, church membership doubled from 1,500 to 3,000 worshipers. In 1924, construction began on a new church; by the end of the 1920s, 4,413 people attended services at St. Lawrence. Yet the church remained unfinished. Fundraising, always difficult in the poor congregation, became virtually impossible during the Depression. In the meantime, parishioners celebrated mass in the church basement, the only completed portion of the building. The basement ceiling, protruding slightly above ground level, allowed congregation members to travel down either of two short sets of stairs, passing a small niche built for the organ and choir, into the "basement church."

Reverend Julius Slapsak, ordained in Slovenia in 1925, accepted an assignment to St. Lawrence in 1932. There, he assisted recently arrived immigrants. He remained at St. Lawrence until his transfer in 1964 to St. Vitus Church. Slapsak had always desired to be reassigned to his homeland. He declined membership in the Cleveland Catholic Diocese, choosing to remain a priest in Slovenia's Archdiocese of Ljubljana.

Left: Father Oman, St. Lawrence's pastor for forty-seven years, is shown at the church altar. *Courtesy of Frances "Tanny" Babic.*

Below: In 1929, children participate in the "May Crowning" (a Catholic devotion to the Virgin Mary) in the dark "basement church." *Courtesy of Frances "Tanny" Babic.*

Slapsak retired in 1973; a dozen years later, he died without ever returning to Slovenia.

For decades, the St. Lawrence congregation each year eagerly awaited two special church days, Holy Saturday and the Feast of Corpus Christi. On the Saturday prior to Easter Sunday (Holy Saturday), neighborhood residents brought baskets of food to St. Lawrence to obtain a special blessing and then consumed the food on Easter morning, either before or after a solemn high mass beginning at 5:00 a.m. Also on Holy Saturday, neighborhood boys distributed "Holy Fire" (embers from a controlled fire in the church) to parish homes. Following a blessing in the church, the hot embers would be placed in tin cans with attached wire handles. The makeshift handles protected the boys' hands from the extremely hot cans. In addition, the boys used the wires to twirl the cans through the air to reignite embers that had started to cool. Families initially placed the ashes in their coal stoves and, as the years passed, into more modern gas burners.

More than five hundred colorfully dressed parishioners typically participated in the annual Feast of Corpus Christi in late May or June. Following the 11:00 a.m. mass, the St. Lawrence Church band accompanied a procession that meandered through the neighborhood streets; participants sang traditional Slovenian hymns and recited the Holy Rosary. Curbs, poles

The 1928 St. Lawrence Corpus Christi Day procession passes whitewashed telephone poles as it marches down East Eighty-Second Street. *Courtesy of Special Collections, Michael Schwartz Library, Cleveland State University.*

In the early 1920s, members of a St. Lawrence Church eighth-grade graduating class pose with Father Oman. Ludwic Kuznik (*top right*) later served as a priest at St. Mary in Collinwood. He died in a drowning accident. *Courtesy of Special Collections, Michael Schwartz Library, Cleveland State University.*

and tree trunks had already received a coat of whitewash to symbolize purification. The walk included frequent stops to pray and offer blessings at homes along the route where small alters had been assembled on front porches. Parishioners staged unofficial and friendly competitions to create the most attractive altar. Residents on each street also erected a capelsa (chapel) consisting of an altar and a statue of the Blessed Mother or a favorite saint. Eventually, buses transported parishioners from nearby Slovenian churches to participate in the celebration.

On September 24, 1939, the congregation laid the cornerstone for the new church to be constructed on top of the basement church. Nearly one year later, several thousand people knelt in the street in front of the new brick Romanesque house of worship with stone trim to receive a blessing and celebrate the church dedication and the consecration of the Italian marble altar. An unusual ceiling of wood panels, beautifully decorated with ecclesiastic symbols and portraits of the apostles, became a striking focal point of the new church, which serviced eight hundred families with a capacity for seven hundred parishioners at each mass. The

Father Oman is surrounded by a 1939 communion class in front of the church rectory. *Courtesy of Frances "Tanny" Babic.*

Slovenians' love for music manifested itself in a different choir singing at each Sunday mass. The singing groups consisted of adults, separate choirs composed of females and males in their twenties and a youth choir. Years later, priests still delivered sermons in the Slovenian language.

In 1945, exiled bishop Gregory Rozman fled Ljubljana because of his opposition to both the Nazi and Communist occupations of Yugoslavia. The communists sentenced him in absentia to eighteen years of hard labor because of his hostility toward their regime. In 1948, Rozman established his residence in the St. Lawrence rectory. No stranger to the church, back in 1935, he had preached at St. Lawrence for a full week while conducting a three-month tour of Slovenian churches in the United States. Rozman continued his residence until his death in 1959 at the age of seventy-seven.

During his long career, Father Francis M. Baraga served five northeast Ohio Slovenian churches. In 1935, he transferred from a Youngstown church to St. Mary in Collinwood. From 1944 to 1953, he served St. Vitus Church. He then became pastor of St. Lawrence prior to a 1960 transfer to St. Christine Church in Euclid, Ohio. Baraga returned briefly to St. Lawrence before retiring in 1967.

Slovenian-born Father Joseph Varga replaced Baraga. Varga had entered the United States as a refugee priest in 1952 and served at St.

The exterior of St. Lawrence Church is shown in a postcard. *Courtesy of Special Collections, Michael Schwartz Library, Cleveland State University.*

Mary in Collinwood. Father Anthony Rebol replaced Varga when the latter died in 1979. Rebol performed his first mass at St. Vitus in 1956 and later resided at Holy Rosary Church and St. Mary in Collinwood. In 2002, Rebol retired at the age of seventy-four because of alleged child sexual abuse charges. The Cleveland Diocese never assigned another permanent priest to St. Lawrence Church

Back in 1951, the St. Lawrence congregation had observed the fiftieth anniversary of its founding. Ohio governor Frank Lausche attended the celebration. About eight hundred families belonged to the church at the time. Even in 1962, nearly five hundred parishioners paraded through the neighborhood in the Corpus Christi procession. But the area would soon begin a noticeable decline.

During the final two decades of the twentieth century, the number of parishioners plummeted, from more than fourteen hundred to about three hundred. The once-energetic Corpus Christi celebration waned and then temporarily vanished. In 2002, the church revived the festivity, but the mostly elderly congregation could walk for only one block. As the number of parishioners declined even further, the century-old church closed following a farewell mass on June 20, 2010.

3

St. Clair Avenue

Listen for an Accordion

In the first decade of the twentieth century, many Slovenians journeyed to Cleveland with a piece of paper containing the name of a relative or friend and the word "St. Clair." A vicar at St. Vitus Church is credited with providing immigrants with this advice for reaching Cleveland's St. Clair Slovenian neighborhood: "In the center of the city, on Public Square, stop and wait until the carriage of the street train with 'St. Clair Avenue' written on it comes by. Get in and ride the street train until you hear the sound of an accordion. Then you shall have arrived among Slovenes."

Similar to Newburgh, the St. Clair area offered immigrants employment in a variety of factories and mills. The neighborhood derived strength from the many laborers who turned into long-term residents. Anthony Kosan Sr., a millwright at the Eaton Corporation, lived in the area for sixty-eight years and literally married the girl next door. Frank Bencina, a machinist for the Cleveland Railway (streetcar) Company, resided on East Sixtieth Street for nearly half a century. Mathija Dulc worked at the United States Pipe Company from his 1889 arrival until his 1932 retirement. James Bartol labored for thirty-eight years as a motorman for the St. Clair Avenue streetcar line. John Korosec demonstrated why Slovenians earned a deserved reputation as reliable employees. Living on East Thirty-Ninth Street, Korosec walked a round-trip of about twelve miles each day to his first job, located in Collinwood.

Many family-owned businesses, prospering for decades, contributed to the neighborhood's stability. In 1903, Joseph Zalokar opened a café on Addison

The Norwood Food Market (*background*) provided groceries for the neighborhood. This image is from 1954, just prior to the closing of the market. *Courtesy of Special Collections, Michael Schwartz Library, Cleveland State University.*

Road; sixty-one years later, he suffered a stroke in the café and died the same day. Anton Martincic operated a grocery store on Prosser Avenue for thirty-five years until his death in 1952. Dr. Frank Seliskar immigrated to St. Paul, Minnesota, in 1897. After earning a medical degree from Western Reserve University, he opened an office at St. Clair Avenue and East Sixty-Second Street, where he accommodated patients for decades. Mattias Ermakora operated a St. Clair Avenue tailor shop for thirty years.

Frank Cerne peddled merchandise in several cities prior to settling in Cleveland in 1903 at the age of twenty-eight. In 1909, he founded a small store on St. Clair Avenue, originally selling jewelry, watches and diamonds. Cerne soon added phonographs and, through the decades, ushered in a large selection of electrical appliances. In the 1920s, the store carried radios and wringer-less electric washers along with safety razors and fountain pens. At the onset of the Great Depression, Westinghouse cabinet-model radios sold for $112 to $350. Following a bankruptcy in 1932, Cerne regrouped with an even larger St. Clair Avenue store. The late 1940s witnessed the debut of electric coffee makers. Electric shavers headed the list of 1950s additions; electric hair dryers debuted in 1960. Following Frank's retirement, his son Howard and Howard's wife, Eleanor, took over the business, which continued into 1969.

Jerry Bohinc, born in 1905 in Cleveland to Slovenian parents, immigrated to Slovenia at the age of five. Thirteen years later, he came back to Cleveland, settling in the St. Clair Avenue neighborhood. He worked for the American Electric Steel Company and then General Electric during the Depression. In 1931, after being laid off from General Electric, Bohinc loaded a trailer filled with gas stoves and followed East Ohio Gas installation crews to suburban worksites. He traveled door-to-door, demonstrating new gas stoves to families about to receive gas service for the first time. He soon accumulated enough money to establish the Norwood Appliance Store in the St. Clair Avenue neighborhood and a second business on Waterloo Road in Collinwood. In 1947, he founded the Northeast Appliance and Furniture Store on Lakeshore Boulevard. Bohinc and his four sons built the company into an eight-store chain. In 1989, they sold the business to a San Francisco–based leveraged buyout firm.

Slovenian immigrant Louis Cimperman arrived in Cleveland in 1907. Twenty-one years later, he purchased a grocery store and meat market on Glass (now Lausche) Avenue, later moving the shop to Norwood Avenue. When Louis died in 1949, his wife, and later his son, continued the business into the 1990s.

One St. Clair Avenue business, despite considerable changes in the neighborhood, is now in its fourth generation of family ownership. In 1938, Ignatius (Ignace) Slapnik opened a flower shop (6102 St. Clair Avenue) in the former site of a Slovenian cooperative grocery store. In the 1940s, Ignatius's son Louis took over the business, followed by Ignatius's grandson Donald and his wife, Nancy. The company still exists, now operated by Ignatius's great-granddaughter Shelli and her mother, Nancy.

James, another son of Ignatius, founded a florist business about five blocks east of his father's store (6620 St. Clair Avenue). Born in Slovenia in 1909, James came to Cleveland as a child. He operated the shop from the 1930s to 1956, when he died at the age of forty-seven in his home above the store. His son James Jr. continued the business into the 1990s.

In 1942, Charles, a third son of Ignatius, opened another nearby florist business (6026 St. Clair Avenue). In 1960, Charles (then fifty-three years old) died in the kitchen of his home situated above the store. Just a few

The Slapnik Flower Shop, shown here in 1961, still exists on St. Clair Avenue. *Courtesy of Cleveland Public Library, Photograph Collection.*

months earlier, his forty-seven-year-old wife had died. The site later housed a barbershop.

In the twentieth century's first decade, the St. Clair Avenue neighborhood had surpassed Newburgh as Cleveland's largest Slovenian settlement. In 1910, Slovenians owned nineteen saloons, twelve shoe shops, nine grocery stores, four tailor shops, three butcher shops, pairs of confectioneries, hardware stores and furniture stores, and a barbershop, a bike shop and a savings and loan. These businesses ended the reign of many German establishments that had previously catered to Slovenians and, in the process, created friction between the two nationalities.

A 1905 incident demonstrated the intense competition between local tavern owners and patrons' loyalty to a particular saloon. Counterfeit two-dollar bills had been circulating in the vicinity of East Fifty-Fifth Street and St. Clair Avenue. Two saloonkeepers, Anton Shepic (owner of a drinking place on East Fifty-Fifth Street at St. Clair Avenue) and Louis Lausche (proprietor of a saloon on St. Clair Avenue at East Sixty-First Street), had already engaged in longstanding feuds. On the afternoon of April 24, Lausche informed a U.S. deputy marshal by the name of Sampsell that he had detained Mike Sterle for attempting to pass a fake two-dollar bill. Sterle maintained that he had received the bill the evening before at Anton Shepic's place of business.

Sampsell, not fully appreciating the spirited rivalry between the two drinking places, ordered Lausche and Sterle to accompany him on a six-block journey to Shepic's saloon. As the trio entered, patrons greeted Lausche with cries of "Kill him!" and "Shoot him!," believing the saloon owner intended to create trouble for Shepic. Following the crowd's "wild rush" at Lausche, Sampsell pulled his revolver and threatened to arrest every man in the tavern. He then assisted Lausche in his retreat to his own tavern. A Secret Service agent later released Sterle and Shepic following an interrogation.

During World War I, neighborhood residents petitioned Cleveland to provide a facility for bathing. Built in 1920, the bathhouse later expanded to include a pool and gymnasium. In 1978, a conversion of the old bathhouse developed into the Edward J. Kovacic Recreation Center, which hosts dances, basketball games and swimming and lifesaving instruction. A recent online review captures the essence of the current facility: "The building is old and tired, but the bright smiles from the friendly staff freshen it up."

By the 1920s, most employees of banks, drugstores and retail shops could converse in English, although Slovenian remained the preferred and most comprehended language for communication. As the neighborhood grew, it eventually encompassed much of St. Clair Avenue between East Thirtieth and East Seventy-Ninth Streets, along with side streets intersecting the main thoroughfare.

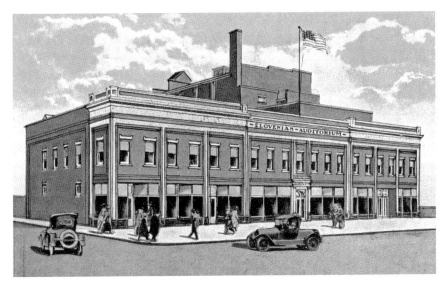

An old postcard provides an early image of the Slovenian National Hall. *Courtesy of the author.*

Because early Slovenian immigrants did not possess a good command of the English language, they preferred to meet with their fellow countrymen in pubs and small halls near their homes. In 1903, they began collecting funds to construct a meeting place of their own. The next year, Jerney Knaus opened the new Knaus Hall on St. Clair Avenue and temporarily ended the fundraising efforts. Knaus had immigrated to Cleveland from Slovenia in 1892 and headed a dairy company and grocery store.

In 1914, Slovenians renewed their efforts to build a new meeting place because of the increase in population and in social and cultural activities. Contributors who accumulated ten dollars' worth of stamps (sold by merchants in small denominations) received one share of ownership in the yet-to-be-built structure. Slovenian leaders also offered stock for sale at meetings, banquets, parties and other social gatherings. Societies and organizations expecting to reside in the building also contributed to the construction fund. But in 1918, available cash had declined somewhat from the year before because a portion of the contributions had been directed toward supporting the war effort. Also, the number of public meetings had declined due to the Spanish flu epidemic. Efforts to construct the new building continued for another five years.

Finally, on April 15, 1923, the neighborhood celebrated laying of the cornerstone. Three thousand exuberant marchers, many wearing national costumes of velvet and satin spangled with gold and silver braid and tassels, joined three bands in a parade extending more than a half mile. On March 1, 1924, the national home opened with a 1,228-seat auditorium, two meeting halls, a gymnasium, a library and commercial storefronts.

Through the years, the hall has hosted singing and dancing programs, operas, recitals, meetings, conventions, political rallies, union gatherings, banquets, wedding receptions, clambakes, boxing matches, weight-lifting tournaments and Buddhist and Japanese food bazaars.

A Cleveland Public Library branch also provided Slovenians with a place to meet their neighbors, discuss politics and obtain news from their homeland. For new immigrants, the library played a vital role in bridging gaps between their Austrian culture and the American way of life.

Located at the corner of East Fifty-Fifth Street and St. Clair Avenue, the library offered books, periodicals and newspapers written in the Slovenian language. In 1937, the branch still stocked 3,546 books published in the Slovenian language. The most popular volumes included *A Tale of Two Cities*, *Oliver Twist*, *Tom Sawyer*, *Tarzan of the Apes* and the works of James Fenimore Cooper. Talented first-generation Americans presented concerts and recitals

The St. Clair Avenue branch of the Cleveland Public Library, located at the intersection of East Fifty-Fifth Street, provided books and cultural events into the early 1940s. *Courtesy of Cleveland Public Library Archives.*

in the Slovenian language. Looking to the future, the library also offered classes in beginning English and citizenship.

In 1941, when the library relocated to three converted storefronts on St. Clair Avenue, the *Plain Dealer* proclaimed, "Mr. Frank T. Shadolnik will be its librarian. This will mark the first time in the history of the Cleveland Public Library that a branch will be headed by a man." The library served neighborhood Croatians and Lithuanians as well as Slovenians.

For decades, Slovenian culture pervaded family life during church holidays and weddings. Even into the 1940s, Slovenian families celebrated Christmas with distinctive rituals. On Christmas Eve, the evening meal, served on a white tablecloth, included freshly baked bread and the finest foods that the family could afford. Later, the family often attended midnight mass. The father led the procession if the family walked to church.

On Christmas morning, the entire family participated in a procession that encompassed every room in the home. Carrying a bowl of holy water, the household's oldest woman, most often a mother or grandmother, led the procession. Children carried lighted candles as the family blessed each room. The father placed a lighted candle on the Christmas tree to conclude the ritual. The family then sang Christmas carols while opening gifts.

Shaw's Billiards and the building to the right became part of the Cleveland Public Library's Norwood Branch in 1941. *Courtesy of Cleveland Public Library Archives.*

In the early 1960s, single three-bedroom homes in the neighborhood sold for $9,500; two-family double homes commanded $14,500. For those desiring to rent, an apartment building on Bonna Avenue offered a five-room suite for $70 per month. Within ten years, the freshly painted homes and neat yards were almost surrounded by vacant and decaying factory buildings and a growing, crime-ridden slum. By 1970, vandals had damaged much of the neighborhood's Grdina Park. Yet, many Slovenians remained committed to a neighborhood that still offered considerable advantages—family, friends, St. Vitus Church, the Slovenian National Home, grocery stores, meat markets and a seven-minute bus ride into downtown Cleveland. In the 1970s and '80s, businesses remained profitable while residents enjoyed evening walks through the neighborhood.

But in the 1990s, fear of crime had developed into a constant anxiety. Heavy metal fences surrounded many well-kept yards; nearby, drug dealers operated from otherwise empty homes. Rumors that a prison and halfway house would be constructed on East Fifty-Fifth Street created concerns. Yet, as the neighborhood turned tougher, so did its residents and business proprietors. In 1994, when a robber attempted to hold up a family-owned bakery located in the Slovenian National Home since 1943, storekeeper Gertrude Nosan, who possessed near-perfect hearing, asked the assailant to speak louder because she had trouble understanding him. Totally frustrated,

In 1951, two young readers enjoy examining books at the Norwood Public Library. *Courtesy of Cleveland Public Library Archives.*

the man journeyed down the street, attempting to rob a nearby bookstore instead. When owner Ivan Vzeba claimed he had no money, the annoyed villain pushed him aside, but directly toward the door. Vzeba used this opportunity to escape in search of help, leaving the criminal with the task of unlocking a secured cash register. He was unsuccessful. On his third robbery attempt, the man managed to make off with a small amount of cash from a bank on the same block. Some witnesses claim the scoundrel had actually robbed the bank first and remained on the street while attempting the two other holdups.

Later in 1994, two incidents tested the tenacity of even the most resolute residents as thugs preyed on elderly Slovenians still living in the area. A mugger followed eighty-seven-year-old Theresa Klemen home from her trip to a grocery store. The assailant shoved her to the ground, stuffed her scarf into her mouth and snatched her purse. Although mentally shaken, she sustained only minor injuries.

When Stanislav Mrva died, his wife, Marija (a cousin of Theresa Klemen), vowed to remain in the neighborhood. Three weeks after Klemen survived her attack, eighty-four-year-old Marija died in her home at the hands of a brutal murderer who administered several blows to her head and stabbings to her back, face and hand. St. Vitus pastor Joseph Boznar sadly commented in the *Plain Dealer*, "We are becoming prisoners, especially the elderly, in our homes, and I think that reflects the way this neighborhood really is."

In the early twenty-first century, two landmark St. Clair neighborhood Slovenian food stores closed within a few years of each other. Immigrants Anton and Mary Malensek opened their Norwood Road market in 1917. In 1940, Anton's son Gus took over the business. During Christmas season in the 1940s and '50s, the family sometimes sold more than five thousand links of sausage in one day. In 1969, Gus's son Ken became the third-generation owner. He had worked in the market his entire life. His brother Tom entered the business a year later. All three generations had lived in a house attached to the market through the home's kitchen. After eighty-seven years, the market closed in 2004.

In 1944, Frank and Frances Longar launched their market near the corner of East Fortieth Street and St. Clair Avenue. The family also lived in a home attached to the store. Frances bore more of the responsibilities for running the market while her husband worked as a machinist at Cleveland Twist Drill. She spoke both Slovenian and Croatian, often conversing with customers in either language. Following Frank's death in 1976, Francis (the son of Frank and Frances) and two granddaughters stepped in to help operate the store. All three worked in the market before they had reached the age of ten. In 2000, Francis died at the age of eighty-seven, and the market closed shortly afterward.

Although no longer dominated by Slovenians, the area is making a very robust comeback. Today, a larger St. Clair–Superior district (which

Kurents parading down St. Clair Avenue chase away winter doldrums and hasten the arrival of spring. *Courtesy of St. Clair Superior Development Corporation.*

Dancing on St. Clair Avenue and in the Slovenian National Hall are highlights of the annual Kurentovanje celebration. *Courtesy of St. Clair Superior Development Corporation.*

includes the old Slovenian neighborhood) is home to a diverse and growing population of about ten thousand residents who collectively speak twenty-three different languages or dialects.

One of the more creative new businesses in the area is Cleveland Flea, a monthly bazaar-type event highlighting local small business. It draws about 170 vendors and thousands of shoppers to each session. The "Hub 55" project has added a café and microbrewery to the East Fifty-Fifth Street neighborhood. A two-day AsiaTown festival attracts about fifty thousand people each year, and an annual Ingenuity Fest (an art and technology festival) has moved to the area. Asian Night Markets offer food, drink and vendors in the summer months.

While the emerging neighborhood now attracts a variety of ethnic groups, one of Cleveland's fastest growing annual celebrations is entrenched in the area's Slovenian roots. Kurentovanje is a celebration highlighted by lovable ten-foot kurents, mythical monsters that supposedly have the power to chase away winter and welcome spring. The festivities include live music (with a heavy concentration on polkas) and merchants selling beer, food and crafts. A parade beginning at Sterle's Country House continues down St. Clair Avenue to the Slovenian National Home. But the kurents first appear the day before at an equally festive "Kurent Jump," in which the affable monsters dance around a campfire.

4

St. Vitus Church

Where Triumph Overcame Tribulation

Typical of many ethnic neighborhoods, a Catholic church firmly anchored the St. Clair Avenue community. Yet the initial harmony between St. Vitus Church and the area's Slovenians proved to be fragile. Disagreements between the priest and a significant portion of the congregation shook the very foundation of the neighborhood. The conflict began almost immediately following the debut of the church.

Prior to the founding of St. Vitus, Slovenians of the St. Clair neighborhood worshipped at Our Lady of Lourdes, a Bohemian parish located near Broadway Avenue and East Fifty-Fifth Street. The arrangement generated its share of drawbacks, including a burdensome commute between the two neighborhoods. A communication dilemma arose during the confession ritual, since Slovenian worshipers and Father Stefan Furdek, a Bohemian, did not speak each other's language with consistent fluency.

Joseph Turk, the former Newburgh neighborhood activist, suggested that priests from the Slovenian portion of Austria be imported to serve in Cleveland. The local bishop opposed this idea, largely because he believed priests already established in Europe would have difficulty adjusting to American customs. In addition, an imported priest would remain under the jurisdiction of the Austrian Empire.

As a compromise, the bishop recommended importing theological students from Europe who would complete their studies in the United States, in the process becoming more familiar with the English language and American conventions. During a trip to Bohemia and Slovakia, Furdek arranged a side excursion to Slovenia, where he recruited Vitus Hribar to serve the St. Clair Avenue Slovenians.

Ordained in 1893, the twenty-three-year-old Hribar celebrated his first masses at Our Lady of Lourdes. That year marked the founding of the St. Vitus parish, the first church specifically devoted to Slovenian Catholics in the United Sates. Lacking a physical building, the congregation began by worshiping in St. Peter's Church in downtown Cleveland. Meanwhile, the local Catholic diocese purchased land on the corner of Norwood Road and Glass (later Lausche) Avenue and, in 1894, dedicated a small wooden church to St. Vitus in honor of its first priest. Reflecting the immigration patterns of the time, the initial church membership consisted of sixty-five families and more than nine hundred unmarried men.

The young, recently ordained priest faced difficult challenges in founding a new parish. In 1905, a serious discord developed between Hribar and the parishioners, partly created by the congregation's lack of understanding regarding the funding of church maintenance in America. In Austria, the government paid for the maintenance of churches and religious schools, along with caring for the needs of the priests. In America, the congregation assumed these responsibilities, sometimes at significant sacrifice to the parishioners. St. Vitus worshipers rebelled when Hribar requested contributions toward building maintenance.

Parishioners also criticized Hribar for his indifference or opposition to the formation of church groups and organizations, apparently seeking to retain total control of the parish. Hribar's problems accelerated when the congregation accused him of availing himself of church funds for his personal use. Church members chastised him for charging thirteen dollars to perform a marriage ceremony while refusing to spend church funds on picnics and social affairs. Anton Grdina, the church treasurer, confronted Hribar regarding spending issues and promptly lost his job. In addition, Hribar's staunch vocal opposition to drinking liquor did not endear him to all church members. The influential Slovenian newspaper *Nova Domovina* characterized Hribar as a "bad and greedy priest." Hribar later served northeast Ohio churches into the mid-1950s with no further accusations of being greedy, bad or dishonest.

Meanwhile, prominent church member Louis Lausche had convinced Father Kazimir Zakrajsek to emigrate from Slovenia. The malcontent portion of St. Vitus assumed that the hand-picked Zakrajsek would replace Hribar. But the embittered priest fought back by founding *Danica*, a newspaper dedicated to both refuting the claims against him and expressing negative views toward Zakrajsek.

Demanding the transfer of Hribar and the promotion of Zakrajsek, an angry crowd marched three miles from St. Vitus to the downtown St. John's Cathedral rectory home of the bishop. Protesters carried "Down with Fr. Hribar" signs while a band and several red-shirted men on horseback entertained curious onlookers. Although the protestors notified the bishop well in advance of the date and time of their planned march, on their arrival, a priest informed them that the bishop could not be located. The activists then decided to partake in a side trip to Cleveland mayor Tom L. Johnson's Euclid Avenue residence, where they demanded the ouster of their priest. Immigrants assumed that Johnson would directly intervene in the dispute since, unlike in the United States, mayors in Slovenia possessed such powers. During the demonstration, police arrested a few protestors, charging them with disturbing the peace and threatening Hribar.

The following week, militant church members, clad in khaki suits and carrying rifles, staged a second march. A priest at the cathedral informed the group that no meeting with the bishop would take place. Organizing yet another demonstration, the malcontent group threatened to remain at the cathedral until the bishop took notice of their demands. But instead of a welcoming priest, twenty uniformed patrolmen and a contingent of detectives and plainclothesmen greeted the protestors, ending the threatened church siege before it began.

In addition to the futile downtown marches, combative church members staged acts of violence during a three-year period of turmoil. Early in the St. Vitus chaos, Hribar discovered the doors to his church nailed shut while a belligerent mob shouted threats as they surrounded him. He also received intimidating letters, one of which read, "Resign or take the consequences." His supporters volunteered to guard the rectory during the evening hours.

On another occasion, a drunken man stood in front of the parish rectory, shouting vile names at the priest. Other rowdies joined in from nearby saloons and rooming houses, swelling the crowd to about two hundred. The gang, unsuccessful at storming the rectory doors, did manage to throw a brick through the priest's window.

Less than two weeks later, another outbreak of violence occurred when police attempted to disburse a crowd gathered around the rectory. The mob showered the police with stones and bricks. Members of the crowd continued fighting even after being clubbed in the head with police nightsticks. The wife of a victim attacked a policeman, attempting to smear the officer with the blood flowing from her husband's badly cut head.

In 1906, Bishop Horstmann finally took action, separating the parish into two parts, with East Fifty-Fifth Street the dividing line. To the west, the bishop created a new parish, Our Lady of Sorrows, headed by Zakrajsek. The church temporarily conducted services at Ullman's Hall, a meeting place on East Fifty-Fifth Street that came equipped with an attached saloon. The church soon moved to a storefront on East Forty-First Street near St. Clair Avenue. The unpopular Hribar remained at St. Vitus.

The dual-parish arrangement resulted in the two priests engaging in a spiteful feud, accusing each other of lies and slander. Zakrajsek also claimed that Francis L. Kerze, the St. Lawrence Church priest in Newburgh, had meddled in the affairs of the quarrelling churches. Zakrajsek correctly warned the bishop that failure to address these smoldering issues would result in more disorder and scandals. Yet the bishop's difficult decisions led to even more disorder.

Horstmann transferred Hribar to Barberton, Ohio, and Zakrajsek to Lorain, Ohio (and soon to New York). He chose Reverend Bartholome Ponikvar as the new St. Vitus priest and Casamir Stefanic, newly ordained to the priesthood, to Our Lady of Sorrows. Both appointments were met with vehement opposition. Eight hundred St. Vitus members adopted a hostile resolution: "Rev. Bartholome Ponikvar will not be allowed to take possession of St. Vitus Church." The declaration also rejected Stefanic in advance, just in case the bishop would consider that option. But at the request of Zakrajsek, the St. Vitus Parish reluctantly accepted Ponikvar.

Born in Slovenia in 1877, Ponikvar arrived in the United States in 1901; five years later, he celebrated his ordainment. On August 2, 1907, Ponikvar began his service at St. Vitus. The new priest proved to be an excellent healer for the parish and remained its leader for forty-four years and eight months, until he died in his sleep in 1952.

Unfortunately, the transfer of Zakrajsek enraged the Our Lady of Sorrows congregation, greatly worsening its situation. A significant faction declared that it would return to Ullman's Hall rather than continue under Stefanic. Not long afterward, a group of disorderly men sang, danced and cheered while using hammers to wreck the church sanctuary and batter its beautiful gold chalices. The rowdy group defaced holy pictures with red paint, strewed broken glass over the carpets and trampled the altar cloths and linens. At the next scheduled mass, Stefanic conducted the service accompanied by police protection.

Stefanic accused the malcontent members who had seceded from the church of the destructive acts. Yet others blamed the priest's own supporters for the violence, claiming they hoped to obtain sympathy from the bishop. Five hundred members of the church felt strongly enough to draft a letter to the bishop accusing the Stefanic supporters of the criminal action.

The dilemmas that street fights and church politics failed to solve ended up in the hands of attorneys. Anton Grdina brought a lawsuit against Fathers Kerze and Hribar, claiming libel because of an article written in a newspaper published by the two priests. Representing the other side of the conflict, police arrested Raymond Feigel, the editor of *Nova Domovina*, a daily newspaper published on St. Clair Avenue, on charges of criminal libel following a complaint by Father Kerze. He alleged that the paper had printed an article about him filled with "venomous attacks."

Three years of church warfare finally concluded when Our Lady of Sorrows ran out of money. In addition, all of the priests involved in the conflict realized that continuation of the discord would serve no useful purpose. Members of Our Lady of Sorrows requested reinstatement at St. Vitus.

In 1922, Vitus Hribar became pastor at St. Mary Church in Collinwood. He served three successful decades there. One day, he lost his balance in the parish rectory and suffered a back injury that prevented him from active

The dramatic interior of St. Vitus Church is shown in a current photograph. *Courtesy of the author.*

participation in mass. He died in 1956 at the age of eighty-six.

After its initial traumas, St. Vitus settled into a remarkable period of expansion combined with pastoral stability. In 1915, the parish had grown to a membership of about eighty-five hundred worshipers, the largest Slovenian parish in the United States.

During the Depression, the St. Vitus congregation constructed a new church on Glass (now Lausche) Avenue at East Sixty-First Street. Representing an extraordinary sacrifice from a devoted congregation, the dedication took place in 1932, when about 30 percent of the Slovenian workforce remained unemployed. The exterior is constructed with yellow brick highlighted by ivory tile ornamentation. The interior features

Born and raised in the St. Vitus neighborhood, Reverend Louis Baznik headed the church for seventeen years. *Courtesy of Cleveland Public Library, Photograph Collection.*

arched ceilings and seating for more than one thousand worshipers. East and west galleries add space for another four hundred people.

Father Louis B. Baznik, no stranger to the neighborhood, replaced Ponikvar when the latter died in 1952. Baznik's father had been one of the founders of St. Vitus; as a child, Baznik served as an altar boy assisting Ponikvar. After attending the parish school, he graduated from Cathedral Latin High School and entered a seminary. Ordained in 1935, Baznik first conducted mass at St. Lawrence Church and then as an army chaplain. In 1960, after seventeen years at St. Vitus, he contemplated semiretirement and requested a transfer to St. Patrick Church in Geauga County. His new church consisted of about two hundred families (one-tenth the size of St. Vitus). In 1993, the eighty-five-year-old Baznik died in a nursing home in Euclid, Ohio.

Father Rudolph A. Praznik, a graduate of St. Vitus School, Cathedral Latin High School, John Carroll University and St. Mary Seminary, replaced Baznik. Praznik had been ordained in 1940 and assigned to St. Lawrence Church in Newburgh and was later transferred to churches in Euclid and Barberton (both in northeast Ohio). His relatively short service at St. Vitus ended with his death in 1975.

Born in 1925, Reverend A. Edward Pevec, a child of immigrant parents, also grew up in the St. Vitus neighborhood. Although born in Cleveland, the future priest entered the first grade with virtually no knowledge of the English language. He later demonstrated good southpaw batting and pitching skills on nearby playgrounds. But from an early age, Pevec desired to enter the priesthood. An honor student at Cathedral Latin High School, his 1942 graduating class voted him the "most likely to take a drink." Ordained in 1950, he preached at St. Lawrence Church before becoming a professor at the Borromeo Seminary. In 1975, Pevec returned to his old neighborhood as pastor of St. Vitus, but he soon received a promotion to auxiliary bishop (essentially assistant to the bishop). He served as a priest for sixty-four years and died at the age of eighty-nine. Father Joseph P. Boznar, who joined St. Vitus in 1979, remains as the church pastor.

In 1902, St. Vitus established its first elementary school. By the end of the decade, enrollment reached one thousand students. St. Vitus was soon to reign as the largest Slovenian parish school in the United States. In 1914, the church constructed a new school, on the corner of Norwood and Glass Avenues, with eighteen classrooms for nine grade levels. Thirteen years later, the school accommodated eighteen hundred students. Three-quarters of a century later, in 2003, the school closed due to a lack of students.

5

The East Ohio Gas Fire

A Neighborhood Explodes

As a blistering fireball crashed through the day-old kitchen window of Mary Anne Kolar's newly remodeled home, the five-months-pregnant daughter of Slovenian immigrants whispered a short prayer, grabbed her children and rushed out of the house. Meanwhile, elementary school students at St. Vitus School watched another ball of fire race southward down East Sixty-First Street. To the west, fourteen-year-old Edward Krivacic witnessed an explosion from a window at Willson Junior High School on East Fifty-Fifth Street. The havoc occurred on October 20, 1944. Many members of the Slovenian community initially thought that Germans had bombed Cleveland. But a business located in the heart of the St. Clair neighborhood actually created the incredible blast.

The East Ohio Gas Company stockpiled liquefied gas, cooled to minus 250 degrees Fahrenheit, in four three-story tanks located at the north end of East Sixth-First Street. At this temperature, six hundred times more gas could be stored as compared with traditional storage methods. Hailed as a miracle of engineering simplicity, East Ohio Gas established the facility in 1941 as only the second such installation in the country. The tanks, originally intended as a safeguard against cold winters, soon developed a new purpose as the government hoarded gas for possible wartime use.

An undetermined spark ignited gas leaking from a seam on the side of one of the tanks. The resulting blast created a flame rising 2,800 feet into the air. Charred birds appeared to fall from the clouds while telephone poles blazed like flares. Buildings exploded into bonfires as streets and sidewalks

The 1944 explosion of an East Ohio Gas storage tank containing liquefied gas reduced homes on East Sixty-First Street to flaming skeletal embers. *Courtesy of Special Collections, Michael Schwartz Library, Cleveland State University.*

buckled. Spinning manhole covers soared several hundred feet in the air. The explosion's strength represented about one-sixth of the power of one of the atomic bombs that would soon decimate Japan.

Twenty minutes later, a second tank, buckling from the heat, burst into flames. Gas from the two tanks rushed across twenty city blocks, some of it disappearing into sewer openings, where it mixed with sewer gas and invaded some residential basements while bypassing others. This lethal mixture created even more explosions along many deadly pathways. The temperature at the core of the explosion is estimated to have exceeded three thousand degrees Fahrenheit. The extreme heat vaporized portions of the neighborhood; other segments burned uncontrollably.

Seeking safety from the swelling flames, neighborhood children sprinted forty blocks eastward to East 105th Street. A woman vacated her home clutching two squawking chickens in one hand while leading a child with the other hand. Another woman raced back into her blazing home to retrieve her citizenship papers. Factory workers leaped over six-foot fences or used their bare hands to dig under the barriers in their hurried abandonment of the neighborhood. Intense heat on Lake Shore Boulevard caused terrified drivers to abandon their automobiles and leap into Lake Erie. A student driver near the exploding tanks gained real-life experience in driving under adverse conditions. Three miles to the west, terrified downtown office workers felt their buildings shake.

The flames devastated a square mile of residential, commercial and industrial land, killing 130 people, 73 of them East Ohio Gas employees. Of the victims, 61 suffered burns extensive enough to prohibit identification. The flames' toxic routes completely missed many houses and stores, along with St. Vitus School.

For some of the residents who survived the disaster, the clothes they wore constituted their only remaining possessions. Thousands needed a place to live and a store to purchase household essentials. Willson Junior High School

Bodies are removed from the East Ohio Gas machine shop. *Courtesy of Special Collections, Michael Schwartz Library, Cleveland State University.*

Employees of the County Engineer searched for survivors, bodies and any articles that might help to identify the victims. *Courtesy of Special Collections, Michael Schwartz Library, Cleveland State University.*

served as one of the neighborhood's survivors' camps. Homeless residents slept on army cots in the school's basement gymnasium and in second- and third-floor hallways.

Still wary of banks because of failures in the previous decade, families had hidden cash, coins and war bonds in cookie jars, coffee cans, tobacco tins and lard pails. Residents stashed their life savings, sometimes comprising thousands of dollars, under rugs, behind loose bricks, in attic eaves or in spaces between floors and in basement iceboxes. The devastating fire completely destroyed many of these nest eggs. Replacement currency might be obtained from the Federal Reserve by filing a statement of contents and affidavits of honesty from character witnesses. The most successful claims also included the charred remains of what once constituted money or stocks.

Tension remained high within the neighborhood for several days. Following the first two tank explosions, East Ohio Gas engineers believed that the chance of the other two tanks blowing up represented a "considerable danger." Safety director Frank D. Celebrezze commented, "If they go, we're done for." But the tanks remained stable, allowing engineers to completely drain them within a few days.

Within a few days, much of the initial cleanup work had been completed. *Courtesy of Special Collections, Michael Schwartz Library, Cleveland State University.*

An investigative panel determined that, because of wartime restrictions, not enough steel had been used to construct the storage tanks. An East Ohio Gas spokesperson indicated that the first tank to explode had developed a leak during initial testing immediately after its completion. Following repairs and additional tests, the tank appeared to be safe. The committee also concluded that gas storage tanks should never again be constructed in residential neighborhoods.

In 1945, Cleveland politicians discussed the city's need for urban redevelopment and slum clearance, but they deferred action. Slovenian community leaders, headed by Anton Grdina, organized the private St. Clair–Norwood Community Rehabilitation Corporation to rebuild the neighborhood. Grdina donated $5,000 to the cause; neighbors and merchants added additional funds.

The corporation purchased its initial lot from a man who had been offered five times as much from an industrial company. After buying all of the nearby lots, the company surveyed the land to allow for wider frontages.

Rebuilding the industrial and residential portions of the neighborhood required time and money and took years to complete. *Courtesy of Special Collections, Michael Schwartz Library, Cleveland State University.*

Grdina Park now occupies the site of the two gas tank explosions. *Courtesy of the author.*

East Ohio Gas assisted in rebuilding the community by paying more than $3,000,000 to neighborhood residents and an additional $500,000 to the families of the company workers who lost their lives.

The first anniversary of the horrific explosion marked the beginning of construction of twenty-nine new homes. Later that year, a buyer purchased the first completed home, located on East Sixty-First Street near Carry Avenue. New homes sold for between $9,700 and $15,500. People who had lived in the neighborhood prior to the explosion purchased most of these residences. Since 1949, the two-acre Grdina Park, a neighborhood playground, has occupied the former tank storage site.

6

St. Clair Savings

The Great Robbery Capers

The robbery of a relatively small Slovenian financial institution would normally not make international news. But in 1957, when a trio of criminals held up St. Clair Savings, television viewers in every state and parts of Europe sat mesmerized in front of their sets, watching the very first replay of a bank robbery taken from security camera film.

A history of somewhat bizarre previous robberies motivated St. Clair Savings' management to install the then-novel security devices. In 1939, twenty-seven-year-old Edward Broz used a toy pistol to successfully execute a robbery netting $1,769. Despite his initial success, Edward lacked a well-thought-out getaway plan. Just one block west of the crime, he jumped into John Krause Jr.'s automobile while the shocked twenty-six-year-old driver waited at a traffic light. Edward ordered the motorist to drive away without creating a scene. John passed his own St. Clair Avenue home, located in the next block, and traveled as far as East Fifty-Fifth Street and Perkins Avenue. Losing patience and gaining courage, John drove over a curb, grabbed Edward's toy gun and used it to smash him in the face.

Edward then encountered another formidable and unexpected opponent. John's feisty mother had remained calm, quiet and unnoticed in the back seat until her son executed his daring driving maneuver. She then used her purse to inflict multiple wounds to Edward's head. Suffering numerous cuts on his face and head, Edward decided he had had enough of the abusive Krause family and bolted from the car. But the robber proved no match for John, who brought him down with a flying tackle after a chase of only

Edward Broz's robbery of St. Clair Savings turned out to be easier than his attempted getaway. *Courtesy of Cleveland Public Library, Photograph Collection.*

one block. John held Edward on the ground until police arrived. Prior to the robbery, Edward had roamed the St. Clair Avenue neighborhood while on bail awaiting trial for forgery.

A 1955 robbery began as one of two armed men shouted to St. Clair Savings employees an unoriginal but still very convincing message: "This is a stickup." After herding four employees into the vault, the robbers seized $6,775 from several cash drawers. The crime remained unsolved for several years, until Kurt Schuler confessed to his role in the transgression. His admission of guilt proved a bit perplexing to Cleveland authorities, since Kurt confused the bank's name and location, along with the date of the crime. But the twenty-six-year-old's mistakes seemed reasonable enough, since Kurt and his partner, Brian Cowell, had robbed numerous banks in Cleveland, Toronto and Los Angeles. Their criminal career ended in Germany when a jury found the pair guilty of murdering a German policeman during an attempted bank robbery. Cleveland police matched Kurt's fingerprints with those taken from the St. Clair Savings crime scene, officially closing the ongoing investigation. Meanwhile, Kurt and Brian remained in Germany serving life sentences for the murder.

In 1956, a pair of gunmen set their sights on St. Clair Savings' main vault. As one pointed a gun at the two tellers on duty, the other frantically attempted to unlock a swing gate leading to the vault area. He eventually leaped over the gate and encountered manager Anthony C. Kromer, at the time relaxing while munching on an orange. The two marched into the walk-in vault; the robber ordered Anthony to open a time-lock safe. Anthony carried out the demand without objection but then told the gunman he would have to wait fifteen minutes for the vault to open. This unwanted news earned the manager a slug to the head with a pistol butt.

Unable to penetrate the vault in a timely manner, the robbers turned their attention to the excess supply of money held by the two tellers. The pair of criminals relieved Hermine Vicic of $15,000 and Dolores Mihelick of $12,000, along with another $3,000 taken directly from the two tellers' windows. Content with $30,000, the robbers bound the hands of Anthony, Hermine and Dolores with tape and forced them to lie on the floor while they exited the bank. Once again, a flawed escape plan negated an otherwise successful robbery. Anthony, easily freeing himself from the poorly secured tape, dashed outside in time to obtain the license plate number of the getaway car. Police traced the automobile's ownership to a railroad worker, who told them he had lent the car to a relative currently on bail for committing armed robbery. The police expected that the trial would begin the very next day. Detectives soon discovered the abandoned automobile on East Thirty-Ninth Street near Orange Avenue.

Two months later, law officers captured thirty-seven-year-old ex-convict Vandy Lee Mathews in a Monroeville, Alabama bus station. He refused to cooperate with the FBI in identifying the second robber. Vandy received a twenty-year prison sentence, although he actually served only one year.

A troubled Clevelander originally from Alabama, the teenage Vandy had traveled to Dover in 1937 to visit relatives. There he assaulted a Dover resident with intent to kill and raped the man's twenty-seven-year-old wife. When citizens of Dover threatened to lynch him, authorities sent Vandy back to Cleveland to await trial. Returned to Dover, Vandy (as a precaution against violence) received his sentence under the canopy of an outdoor picnic table in a picturesque grove. He served fifteen years of his prison term.

In 1968, a postmaster observed Vandy suspiciously loitering around a post office in Century, Florida. Vandy pulled a gun when a sheriff's deputy attempted to question hm. The deputy shot him in the stomach. Vandy dropped his gun but reached for a knife. The deputy then ended Vandy's life by shooting him in the head.

On April 12, 1957, the day following the installation of the St. Clair Savings security cameras, what appeared to be a mundane bank robbery developed into an international sensation. Within three hours of the crime, the savings institution's management announced it had implemented secret filming of the holdup and released the footage to newspapers and television stations.

Just before their crime, twenty-four-year-old Steven Ray Thomas, along with Wanda DiCenzi (age nineteen) and Rose O'Donnell (eighteen) shared a lunch table with a Pepsi-Cola Bottling Company truck driver at Sorn's Restaurant, located a block west of St. Clair Savings. Following their meal, Rose and Wanda took a ride in Steven's automobile. He surprised the two women by displaying a .32-caliber Beretta pistol and proclaiming, "Let's rob a bank."

Neither Rose nor Wanda took Steven seriously until he used one hand to cover his face with a handkerchief and the other to grasp the pistol. He pointed his weapon at the bank's four employees and three customers. Wanda calmly stuffed $2,400 into a paper bag while Rose warmed up the getaway car, a 1955 black-and-white Buick borrowed from her boyfriend.

Following the holdup, the trio divided their loot and split up. Steven fled on a bus to Indianapolis. On reaching his destination, a stranger in the bus station, making idle conversation, asked Steven if he had seen the film of yesterday's bank robbery in Cleveland. That evening, in horrified disbelief, Steven sat in an Indianapolis bar observing the movie in which he starred as the bank robber. He took the next bus back to Cleveland to surrender, telling police he had turned to crime because an epileptic condition had prevented him from holding steady employment. Shaking his head, he commented, "I got as far as Indianapolis and those pictures were ahead of me."

Rose promised a sixteen-year-old west side female a payment of fifteen dollars if she would hold a sum of money for safekeeping for a few days. Then Rose and Wanda hitchhiked to a Willoughby motel, where they spent the night. Meanwhile, a detective, also enjoying lunch at Sorn's Restaurant on the day of the robbery, recognized Wanda from the surveillance film. A waitress at Sorn's suggested the police talk with workers at a west side restaurant that Wanda also frequented. Although they did not recognize her name, the employees knew that Wanda had worked at a downtown movie house. A Palace Theater manager provided police with Wanda's name and East Cleveland address. Her parents told police she had been missing for several days.

In the home where Rose resided, detectives discovered a parking ticket that enabled them to identify the getaway car. After viewing a film of the robbery on television, the teenager holding Rose's money telephoned police and turned in the cash. Rose surrendered after police arrested her boyfriend, who had lent her the getaway car. She lamented, "I was going to get married. I suppose that's all off now."

Based on a tip, detectives captured Wanda in a Franklin Boulevard rooming house. Within thirty-six hours, Cleveland police had apprehended all three criminals, each of whom incurred jail terms, although the two females received probation within one year.

In 1958, Cleveland police presented the film and an accompanying lecture at the annual convention of the American Academy of Forensic Sciences, held at the Hotel Carter in Cleveland. The following year, attendees of the International Congress on Comparative Law viewed the movie in Brussels, Belgium. The holdup film entered U.S. pop culture by being shown twice on the television program *You Asked for It*.

In 1962, apparently unaware of the surveillance equipment, three men robbed St. Clair Savings of $13,365. The theft started when one member of the trio yelled to the tellers, "This is it. Hand over all the money." One of the robbers fired a shot over the heads of bystanders engrossed in watching the crime. The bullet settled in a nearby wall. The next day, the American public witnessed another authentic robbery film; newspapers across the country printed pictures of the criminals taken from the security cameras.

After viewing the film and pictures, friends and relatives identified Ellie Davis Jr. (age twenty-five), Leroy Jones (twenty-four) and Willie "Duck" Jackson (twenty-three) as the robbers. A parole officer in California recognized Ellie as a convicted burglar who had been arrested for assault with a deadly weapon. Meanwhile, police checked pawn shops in a successful attempt to trace the bullet lodged in the wall. They determined that Ellie had purchased bullets and a gun the day before the robbery. Police also learned that twenty-year-old Arthur Davis (brother of Ellie) drove the getaway car, a stolen and rather conspicuous 1955 yellow Cadillac convertible.

Recognizing the Cadillac, Missouri police arrested all four criminals at a roadblock. While waiting to be taken back to Cleveland, two of the captured foursome demonstrated how to dance the Twist to St. Louis newsmen.

Police also charged Ellie Davis Sr., who owned a delicatessen, with concealing stolen money. Detectives discovered the gun used in the robbery and $3,000 in cash hidden in a staircase in the delicatessen, along with $1,000 stashed in a false ceiling. For the first time, a jury watched the film of a bank robbery. All four major criminals received twenty-year jail terms in the Ohio Reformatory.

St. Clair Savings suffered one final novel robbery prior to its merger with Broadview Savings. In 1969, a robber known as the "Pigtail Bandit" handed a threatening note to a teller and escaped with $2,100. Once again, security cameras provided the means to supply newspapers with pictures of the attractive female lawbreaker. Acquaintances identified twenty-three-year-old Jacquelyn Fay Gentry as the felon. Even though Jacquelyn had cut her trademark pigtails, police arrested her within two weeks of the crime.

7

Collinwood

Cleveland's Industrial Powerhouse

The Village of Collinwood, with its vast array of vineyards, once supplied grapes to destinations throughout the United States. The Lake Shore Railroad tracks, which grape growers used to move their product across the country, divided the village into north and south sections. The railroad also generated the momentum for this largely rural farming community to evolve into an industrial powerhouse following its annexation to Cleveland.

In 1874, the Collinwood Rail Yards and Terminal debuted to service seventy-two freight trains that arrived daily. Initially employing about five hundred workers, the facility grew to accommodate more than two thousand people by 1933, many of them Slovenian immigrants, such as John Tomle. He remained working at the rail yards from 1913 until his 1945 retirement.

Employment opportunities at the railroad complex inspired a residential building boom. In 1875, developers subdivided a portion of an old farm into 180 lots for home construction. Buyers purchased sites for their future dream homes with a twenty-five-dollar deposit and eighteen monthly interest-free payments of ten dollars. For the next eight and a half years, the mortgage required only monthly interest payments at 7 percent. At the end of ten years, the buyer acquired the property with a "balloon" payment for the remaining amount.

The railroad tracks that attracted industry and created jobs also transported visitors from Cleveland to the growing village. On weekends, a train accommodating picnickers destined for Collinwood departed from Public Square. Advertising promised "a route encompassing gardens, graperies and groves." Promoters offered "cheap rates" for their stringently defined target market: "Gentlemen and ladies only—no loafers." Meanwhile, Collinwood's newly opened Goodrich Chapel presented a varied selection of concerts and operettas. Cleveland arts lovers boarded a train from downtown that offered free round-trip accommodations for people purchasing a twenty-five-cent admission ticket to the event.

By the turn of the twentieth century, Collinwood had acquired a distinctly Slovenian flavor. In 1902, residential lots sold for seventy-five dollars, obtainable with two dollars down and weekly payments of seventy-five cents. *Plain Dealer* classified advertisements described positions for salespeople with "pep and personality" to sell land in a new Collinwood allotment described as "a good factory neighborhood." The ability to speak Slovenian ranked high among the list of job requirements. Another real estate sales advertisement promised "a big money proposition for men and women who are willing to work, follow instructions and who can speak Slovenian."

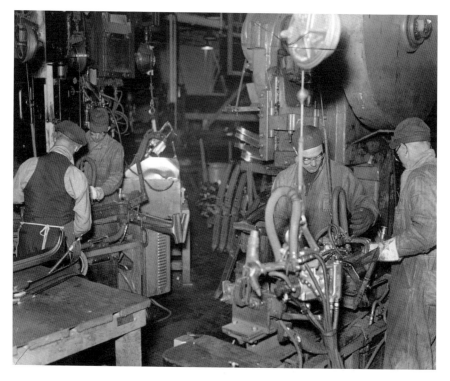

The Fisher Body Plant, depicted here in 1938, provided employment opportunities for many Slovenians. *Courtesy of Special Collections, Michael Schwartz Library, Cleveland State University.*

Ohio's first Slovenian National Home, located on Holmes Avenue, is still an excellent venue for wedding receptions and parties. *Courtesy of the author.*

Inexpensive land and the vast railroad infrastructure motivated industrial companies to build new factories in Collinwood. A Fisher Body plant, debuting in 1921, employed seven thousand workers by 1924. The expanding job opportunities continued to attract Slovenians.

Collinwood's Slovenians initially used the basement of St. Mary Church for their neighborhood meetings and events. On August 24, 1919, they celebrated the opening of Ohio's first Slovenian National Home. Following two remodeling undertakings (in 1927 and 1929), the three-story Holmes Avenue facility, located south of the railroad tracks, continues to incorporate a pub and meeting room for business events on the first floor. The second floor consists of a large auditorium and stage to accommodate plays and concerts. The top floor offers amenities for dances and banquets.

Apparently, members of the home did not endure all of the hardships usually associated with Prohibition. In a 1936 investigation of Cleveland police corruption, officers of the home testified that they had paid thousands of dollars to police during the 1920s to keep beer on tap for their thirsty members.

Through the decades, the Slovenian home has hosted union meetings, political rallies, concerts by local and national singing societies, dramas, operettas, ethnic-oriented conventions, card parties, dances, wedding receptions, banquets, band concerts and weight-lifting contests.

A second meeting place, the two-story Slovenian Workman's Home, soon debuted north of the railroad tracks on Waterloo Road near East 154th Street. During construction, neighborhood Slovenians spent their evenings joining together to form a line from the building site to a nearby brickyard. Passing the bricks from person to person, they formed a "brick brigade" to help reduce transportation costs. The opening ceremonies and events began on September 1, 1926, and continued for three days. The complex initially included an auditorium seating four hundred people, meeting rooms, a recreation area, business offices and a library. A public bar debuted after Prohibition.

Following the addition of a 1939 annex, the Workman's Home added a pub, ballroom, expanded conference rooms, eight bowling alleys, four indoor balina courts, archery facilities and a parking lot. The auditorium's excellent acoustics assisted in booking nationally known opera singers and drama companies. Along with cultural activities, the home has accommodated myriad meetings and events, including minstrel shows, boxing matches,

The Slovenian Workmen's Home on Waterloo Road continues to attract patrons to fish fries, swing dances and polka parties. *Courtesy of the author.*

weight-lifting contests for seniors, socialist clubs, union meetings and the St. Clair Rifle Club.

In the depths of the Great Depression, I.O. Ford, a communist candidate for various public offices, discussed the formation of a farmer-laborer political party. Cleveland's safety director, Eliot Ness, used the Workman's Home to publicly thank the Slovenians who had presented credible evidence that lead to the convictions of several corrupt Cleveland policemen. More recently, in 2011, sixty-seven-year-old Angel Walker, known professionally as Satan's Angel, headlined a burlesque show at the Workman's Home. Recreating her 1960s-era performances, when she advertised herself as the devil's own mistress, Angel simultaneously twirled five tassels, each set on fire. Sold to a private investor in 2016, the home's current ongoing events include wedding receptions, Friday fish fries, Saturday swing dancing and Sunday polka parties.

Luke Tercek emigrated from Slovenia at the age of eighteen and worked for the New York Central Railroad for forty-six years. In 1913, he established Collinwood's first Slovenian cooperative grocery store (where customers purchased a financial interest in the store and received dividends based on its success). By the beginning of World War II, the area supported three such stores, located on East 152nd Street, Waterloo Road and East 200th Street.

August Kollander, a Slovenian immigrant, arrived in Cleveland in 1912. Eleven years later, he established a travel agency on St. Clair Avenue at East 67th Street. Following his death in 1958, new owners relocated the business to East 185th Street, where it serviced Slovenians for decades by booking, among other locations and events, trips to Slovenia and polka festivals throughout the world. The still-existing agency is currently located on East 200th Street. Fulfilling travel requirements for nearly a century, the company has transformed itself from a steamship agency into a business booking chartered jet planes.

In 1928, the Cleveland Public Library opened a Collinwood branch, located at Nottingham Road and East 185th Street, in a former house originally constructed in 1878. Twenty years later, the library moved from the overcrowded home and potential firetrap to a new building on East 185th Street.

Waterloo Recreation, one of Collinwood's longest-running Slovenian establishments, debuted in 1928 on Waterloo Road. Joseph Pozelink and his wife, Angela Grebc Pozelink, both born in the Slovenian portion of Yugoslavia, met in Cleveland and established their combination bar and bowling alley soon after their marriage. Joseph died in 1953, but Angela

Above: In 1940, Mamie Bokal, a clerk in a Slovenian cooperative food store, waited on a customer. *Courtesy of Cleveland Public Library, Photograph Collection.*

Opposite, top: Beginning in 1928, this Nottingham Branch of the Cleveland Public Library served the Collinwood neighborhood for twenty years. *Courtesy of Cleveland Public Library Archives.*

Opposite, bottom: A primary school class in Collinwood's Nottingham School posed for this 1933 picture. *Courtesy of Beth Piwkowski.*

In 1950, a proud Collinwood couple posed next to their Studebaker automobile. *Courtesy of Beth Piwkowski.*

continued running Waterloo Recreation until her death in 1981 at the age of eighty-two. The site later became an art gallery.

While railroad tracks, and later a freeway, separated Collinwood's Slovenian neighborhood, ethnic diversity divided the area in a different manner when a large Italian community settled south of St. Clair Avenue. In the 1920s, many Italian storekeepers told unwanted Slovenian customers that "the Slovenian stores are that way" as they pointed to the north. Even in the 1960s, Slovenian teens avoided Cleveland's Mandalay swimming pool, situated a few blocks south of St. Clair Avenue in an Italian portion of Collinwood. Instead, Slovenians walked to a pool on Avalon Road in Euclid.

Beginning in the 1970s, Collinwood suffered numerous closings of factories that eliminated more than twenty thousand jobs. As land values declined, closed stores and abandoned homes turned into fronts for drug dealers. Forced integration of schoolchildren escalated racial tensions. The rail yards closed as shipments of steel and other materials associated with the automotive industry declined, as did the demand for the finished automobiles. Collinwood Slovenians began an exodus to the suburbs as the neighborhood continued to deteriorate.

By the turn of the twenty-first century, inexpensive live-work accommodations had attracted artists to the neighborhood. Two sections of Collinwood's north side staged impressive comebacks. East 185th Street developed into the site for an annual ethnic street festival that celebrates the Slovenian, Croatian and Lithuanian nationalities. One of the largest street festivals in Ohio, the event focuses on ethnic music (including a dozen polka bands), singers, food, a parade and free polka lessons. More than 200,000 people typically attend the five-day festival, and many return to patronize the shops and restaurants on the street.

On Waterloo Road, the Beachland Ballroom and Tavern debuted in 2000 in the former 1950-vintage Croatian Liberty Home. The venue's success inspired new businesses to locate on a once vibrant but later rundown portion of Waterloo Road. Although no longer specifically attracting Slovenians, the neighborhood has continued to improve.

8

Saint Mary of the Assumption

Collinwood's Slovenian Anchor

By the turn of the twentieth century, the number of Slovenians in Collinwood had grown enough to justify establishment of a Catholic church. But controversy arose over which side of the railroad tracks to locate the new place of worship. The Slovenian population count slightly favored the south: about seventy families and 90 single men lived north of the tracks, and approximately sixty families and 150 unmarried men resided to the south.

The south side argued that Slovaks, Croats and Germans, rather than Slovenians, comprised much of the northern settlement. At the time, the differing ethnicities constituted an important issue in choosing the location for a Slovenian Catholic church. Other ethnic groups had treated Slovenians as outsiders, relegating them to the very back pews at St. Joseph Church, the only Catholic church in Collinwood at the time. In a vote, the south side proponents prevailed—by a margin of only ten ballots.

Prior to the 1906 unveiling of the four-hundred-seat St. Mary of the Assumption Church, located on Holmes Avenue, Reverend Mark Pakiz presided over his first Collinwood mass in his own rented rooms on East 152nd Street. Formal church services began at St. Joseph Church, but the St. Mary congregation soon moved to a nearby hall because of the excessive rent charged by St. Joseph (seventy-five dollars for a Sunday morning service). Almost concurrently, the renegade Saints Peter and Paul independent church, organized by Bohemian priest John Tichy, debuted on the north side of the railroad tracks. After only a few years, the bank holding the church's

This four-hundred-seat St. Mary of the Assumption Church building continued as the Collinwood parish from 1907 into 1958. *Courtesy of Special Collections, Michael Schwartz Library, Cleveland State University.*

mortgage foreclosed. Most of the parishioners grudgingly united with St. Mary. Tichy and a few followers abandoned the Catholic faith altogether.

Pakiz served as Saint Mary's pastor for three years but resigned because of ill health. He later entered the Diocese of Milwaukee. Reverend Anton Smrekar, the next pastor, presided for five years but died of a throat illness. During his funeral service, a thief entered the rectory and absconded with Smrekar's personal manuscripts, including his own poetry and stories. Reverend Paul Hribar celebrated mass at the church for less than five years prior to dying in an accident. The priest and his sister both died instantly when a train struck his automobile. Reverend Joseph Skur then served as pastor for about five years. He spoke Italian as well as Slovenian and English, a very advantageous combination, since Collinwood also housed a significant Italian community. He later became the pastor of a Pittsburgh church. Following these first four rather short pastoral assignments, Reverend Vitus Hribar, who had survived his turbulent residence at St. Vitus Church, guided St. Mary for thirty years.

Membership at St. Mary peaked at nearly six thousand in the mid-1920s. But with the opening of St. Christine Church in Euclid, the number of St. Mary parishioners declined to about thirty-six hundred by 1930.

In 1932, female members of a wedding party pose for a picture prior to the ceremony at St. Mary Church. *Courtesy of Beth Piwkowski.*

During the Great Depression, two associate pastors died in tragic accidents. In 1936, twenty-nine-year-old Reverend Victor Virant had already served at St. Lawrence, St. Vitus and St. Mary. While in Collinwood, he thought he heard prowlers in the rectory and intended to use tear gas to drive them away. After encountering no intruders, Virant put down the tear-gas capsule. The following morning, when the young priest picked up the container, it exploded and killed him. The following year, Reverend Ludwig Kuznik drowned while swimming in Lake Erie.

Activist Reverend Anthony Merkun, ordained in Slovenia in 1900, founded credit unions, farm co-operatives, priest organizations, health centers, homes for the aged and an orphanage in his homeland. In 1945, he immigrated to the United States as a refugee priest when the communists forced him out of Slovenia. The author of twenty books, Merkum spoke six languages fluently but had little initial understanding of English. Beginning in 1947, he resided at St. Mary, where his cousin Reverend Matijar (Matthias) A. Jager served as an assistant pastor. In 1961, Merkum died at the age of eighty-five.

In 1952, Jager replaced the aging and injured Vitus Hribar as St. Mary's pastor. Born in Slovenia and ordained there in 1916, Jager arrived in Cleveland in 1926. Following a fourteen-year assignment at St. Vitus as an assistant pastor, he served at Sacred Heart in Barberton. After fifteen years as pastor at St. Mary, Jager retired in 1967 and moved to Tucson, where he died in 1979 at the age of eighty-five.

In 1957, an extensive fire damaged St. Mary, but repairs permitted its temporary use until a new church, accommodating 830 worshipers at each mass, debuted the next year. The repaired church became a social hall and gymnasium. During the new church's construction, a mystery arose that has remained unsolved to the present day. Following the pouring of the concrete floor, the church janitor vanished and has never been seen or heard from since.

Reverend Victor (Viktor) Tomc, St. Mary's first pastor not born in Slovenia, grew up in the St. Clair neighborhood on Dibble Avenue, south

The new "St. Mary Church" debuted in 1958 and is now nearing its sixtieth anniversary. *Courtesy of the author.*

St. Mary's stunning interior is illustrated in this postcard. *Courtesy of the author.*

of Superior Avenue. After attending St. Vitus Grade School and Cathedral Latin High School, he earned a degree from John Carroll University and studied for the priesthood at St. Mary's Seminary on Ansel Road. In 1943, following his ordainment, he presided at St. Mary, St. Vitus, St. Christine in Euclid and Holy Family Church in Parma, Ohio, before being reassigned to St. Mary to replace Father Jager. Tomc retired in 1987.

The young American-born Reverend John Kumse replaced Tomc. Some members of the parish viewed the new priest with a certain amount of apprehension, concerned that the church's lengthy Slovenian heritage could be at risk. But Kumse quickly alleviated any anxiety by delivering his first mass in Slovenian. Born in Barberton, Ohio, to a Slovenian father and Slovak mother, Kumse spent seven years at St. Vitus Church following his ordainment. After a brief assignment at St. Mary Church in Painesville, he assumed the reins of Collinwood's St. Mary Church.

During his long tenure in Collinwood, members of the church convinced Kumse to take an active part in Cleveland's urban farming movement. Using formerly vacant land near the church, he has become a knowledgeable beekeeper and chicken farmer tending to two hives and eighteen birds. Parishioners even drop notes in the collection basket to order honey or eggs to be purchased the following week.

With the poignant closing of St. Lawrence Church in Newburgh, St. Mary obtained six stained-glass windows from the former Slovenian church. The treasured windows are prominently displayed to the left and right of the altar and in the rear of the church. Today, St. Mary continues to conduct a daily Slovenian mass; weekly church bulletins contain sections printed in Slovenian. Many of the parishioners drive, even on a daily basis, from the nearby suburbs of Euclid and Richmond Heights, to St. Mary. A reasonable number are Slovenian immigrants who entered the United States in the 1960s and '70s.

9

The Collinwood School Catastrophe

The Unimaginable Tragedy

On March 4, 1908, at about 9:30 a.m., sixth-grader Emma Neibert journeyed from her third-floor classroom to a basement washroom. Observing smoke pouring from the basement stairs, she shouted, "The basement is on fire!" to Fritz Hirter, custodian of Lake View School, located in the village of Collinwood on Collamer Street (later East 152nd Street), just south of Lake Shore Boulevard. Following protocol, Hirter sounded the fire alarm (which did not connect to the village's volunteer fire department) and then opened the front and back doors. Unfortunately, the open doors attracted air that rushed through the elementary school, causing an already dangerous fire to escalate in intensity.

The children initially adhered to their already well-rehearsed fire drill practices. But the calmness ended abruptly with the smell of real smoke and the sight of horrific flames. On the first floor, Ethel Rose guided her kindergarten children through a smoke-filled hall to the front stairs, shielding the students by standing with her back to the basement stairway. Although badly burned, Rose remained until all of her class had reached safety, the only students to escape through the front door. Smoke and flames shooting up from the basement quickly rendered the front exit impassible.

Attempting to reach the rear door, fleeing children from the upper floors knocked one another down the narrow steps and through an even more constricted corridor leading to the wide-open back door. In the process, the students jammed tightly on top of each other, creating an impassible barrier to safety. After forming this huge heap of humanity, the children could

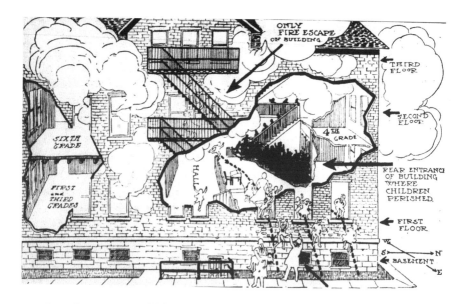

Above: A diagram depicting the rear of Lake View School portrays the school's only fire escape. A cutout illustrates the deadly staircase. *Courtesy of Cleveland Press.*

Left: The mass of children piled up at the rear steps prevented students from exiting the burning school. *Courtesy of Cleveland Press.*

not save themselves nor be saved by teachers, parents or other volunteers. Students trampled their classmates to death; others suffocated in the mound of flesh or died in the flames of the blazing inferno.

Students in Laura Bodey's fifth-grade class, located in the only classroom on the third floor, panicked when they realized obstructions blocked both the front and rear exits. Bodey had worked in the building for only five weeks; she had not yet received training in fire procedures. Yet she calmly directed her class out of the building by using a nearby fire escape. The only deaths in her class arose when a few students did not follow her instructions but, instead, raced to the rear exit. About 80 of the school's 350 children escaped injury; most of the uninjured came from Bodey's and Rose's classes.

Had students in other classes not panicked, they probably would have been led to safety by their teachers. Previous fire drills demonstrated that the building could be evacuated in less than two minutes. Yet the fire claimed the lives of 172 children, 40 of them of Slovenian descent, along with two teachers and a rescuer.

As first-grade teacher Ruby Irwin opened her ground-floor classroom door, smoke and flames racing up the stairs confronted her students. Many unwisely scattered to the front and rear stairs. The children who followed Irwin's instructions retreated into the classroom, where she dropped them from a window to safety. After failing to convince other students to follow her successful exit strategy, she jumped from the window to save herself.

Pearl Lynn, another first-grade teacher with a classroom on the first floor, traveled with her students through heavy black smoke to the blocked back stairway. Smaller children ahead of her had fallen; she stopped so they would have an opportunity to get back on their feet. But sprinting students behind Lynn pushed her down and fell upon her. A member of the school board dragged the unconscious teacher to safety. Without her supervision, all but three of Lynn's students died.

Anna Moran, the school's principal since its 1902 opening, taught sixth grade in a second-floor classroom. Blocked at the staircase by students descending from the third floor, she instructed her students to go back into her classroom and use the fire escape. Unable to open a window leading to a fire escape, she broke it by hurling a chair through the glass. Many of the children did not follow her advice and died attempting to exit from the first floor.

Mary Gollmar, a fourth-grade teacher with a classroom on the second floor, could not navigate her students to the rear stairs. Instead, she directed them to the library and out the fire escape. But very few students

Anna Moran, the school's principal, also taught sixth-grade students. *Courtesy of* Cleveland Press.

followed her instructions. Remaining inside the school, she tried to rescue other students and eventually jumped from a window.

Lula Rowley taught third grade in a second-floor classroom. Although she could not steer her students past the exit door obstacles, Rowley found a first-floor classroom. From there, she dropped the small number of students who obeyed her instructions from a window and then followed them out of the building. The remainder of her students perished as they attempted to exit from the back of the building.

Two teachers died while attempting to save the children's lives. Second-grade instructor Katherine Weiler led her class from the second floor down the rear stairway. The sight of piled-up bodies blocking the exit frightened the children, who tried unsuccessfully to leap over their classmates, in the process making the pile of students even larger. Weiler intentionally hurled herself onto the mound, pleading with the students to use a nearby fire escape. Even with her clothing on fire, the twenty-seven-year-old teacher still tried to pull children from the heap. She and members of her class died from burns, suffocation or being crushed by other students.

On the first floor, Grace Fiske moved her combined first- and third-grade class to a window, where she picked them up and dropped them to safety. As the flames approached, Fiske jumped out herself with two children wrapped in her skirts. She died a few hours later in a hospital.

Terrified parents attempted to pull their children from the mass of bodies or catch them as they jumped from windows or fire escapes. Wallace Upton dragged nineteen children to safety; although he did not realize it, he had pulled his own daughter out of the flames.

But most rescue efforts proved futile. Dying children called in vain to their parents, some standing only a few feet away. The mother of fifteen-year-old Jennie Phillis could not drag her daughter from the mass. She held the child's hands, but Jennie understood the hopelessness of the situation. "It's no use

Teachers Ruby Irwin, Laura Bodey, Ethel Rose, Mary Gollmar and Lula Rowley attended an inquest following the tragic fire. *Courtesy of the* Cleveland Leader.

ma. I've got to die." Her mother stroked her daughter's hair, burning her own hand to the bone before being dragged away.

Mrs. Clark Sprung found her son stretching out his arms for help. The mother ran across the street to her home and secured a stepladder. Climbing up, she reached out and barely caught the boy by his hair. But the fire burned her son's hair off in her hands, and he fell back into the flames to die.

W.C. Schaefer could not free his eight-year-old son George from the tangled heap of suffocating children at the rear door. He temporarily smothered the flames that burned his son's hair, but the fire consumed the boy as his father helplessly watched in utter despair.

Andrew Dorn found his daughter among the mass of children at the back door. He grabbed her arm, but instead of freeing his child, he succeeded only in tearing the arm from its socket.

Some of the terrified children demonstrated extraordinarily heroic behavior. Nine-year-old Niles Thompson successfully leaped from a window but raced back into the building when he realized his younger brother Thomas remained trapped in the blaze. Flames ultimately consumed both boys, an incredible loss to their widowed mother.

Hugh McIlrath, the fourteen-year-old son of Collinwood's police chief, successfully maneuvered himself to a third-floor fire escape. But instead of exiting, he led a group of smaller children down the fire escape. Reaching the bottom, the children needed to jump to the ground; many refused, despite Hugh's efforts. Some of them turned back into the building, and young McIlrath chased after them to induce them to come back. Flames and smoke killed him before he could return to the fire escape.

After escaping by breaking a second-floor window, the badly burned eleven-year-old Oscar Pahner raced to the Collinwood Fire Department to inform them of the horrific fire. When he found no one at the department, he hurried back to the burning school building in an attempt to save his little sister, Edna. Both died in the flames.

Glenn Sanderson, a boy of twelve, met his death in plain view of a large crowd utterly unable to help him. Trapped in the school auditorium on the third floor, Glenn observed the floor beneath him burning. He swung from one piece of auditorium scenery to another, trying to reach the fire escape. Glenn managed to cross the stage about half way, but he missed his grasp and plunged into the fire.

Edna Hebler, a fourteen-year-old student, exited safely from a fire escape. But she climbed back into the building in an attempt to save her six-year-old sister Melba. Edna died on the first floor; meanwhile, Melba had already made her way safely to her home. Fourteen-year-old James Turner had jumped from a window but returned in search of his brothers, Norman (age eight) and Max (six). Rescuers discovered the bodies of all three brothers.

An unidentified girl, about ten years old, protected her little brother, covering his head with her shawl. They both died in the fire. Ten-year-old Mildred Schmitt, her skirts in flames to the knees, ran screaming from the building. She died a few hours later. Three teenaged girls, Mary Ridgeway, Anna Rolth and Gertrude Davis, jumped to their deaths from the third floor while holding hands.

Fire had destroyed the school's interior in fifteen to twenty minutes. Any hope for survival ended when the wooden staircase leading to the upper floors collapsed, sending the children into the burning downstairs coal room. An inadequate village fire wagon, called away from its current task of grading a road, finally arrived at the fire scene. None of the firefighters' ladders could penetrate the second floor. Water from the gasoline-powered pump could not reach the second floor; the feeble streams of water quickly turned into ineffectual steam. The firefighters brought no axes to break down the restraining doors. The village fire chief, out of town at the time of the fire, could not help. But none of this mattered, since the blaze had consumed the school before the personnel and equipment arrived.

Flames at the front of the building quickly made this exit impassible. *Courtesy of Special Collections, Michael Schwartz Library, Cleveland State University.*

Ambulances transported the children's bodies to a temporary morgue established in a Lake Shore Railroad warehouse. Laid out in rows of ten, woolen blankets covered the bodies while a tag denoted the sex of the child. A railroad employee and police officer guarded each row. Parents, admitted ten at a time, attempted to identify their dead children. Mothers attired in furs mingled with women in calico wearing shawls thrown over their heads. Males and females from vastly differing social and ethnic groups consoled one another, grasped each other's hands and shed tears for all the lost children. Mothers fainted, and fathers cursed as they examined bodies now bearing little resemblance to humans. Parents often identified their children by some external object: a silver watch or green marble; a ring, bracelet, buckle or pocketknife; a tooth filling or a fragment of clothing.

The anguished community endured three days of funerals and burials. As somber processions made their way from churches to cemeteries, morbidly curious onlookers peered through the windows of the victims' homes and even pushed their way into some of the houses.

By the time the fire reached its height, no hope remained for saving the children. *Courtesy of the author.*

Fritz Hirter, the forty-six-year-old school custodian, had immigrated to Cleveland from Switzerland. He saved the lives of many students by helping them exit the schoolhouse through windows. Sadly, three of his eight children perished in the fire: Walter (age fifteen), Helena (thirteen) and Ida (eight). Hirter discovered Helena alive but could not pull her free and watched her die in the flames. She had not missed a day of school in seven years. Walter Hirter escaped from the flames but returned to save Ida; the fire killed both of them.

Without any evidence, rumors quickly spread that Hirter's carelessness had caused the fire. Parents accused him of not sounding the fire alarm in a timely manner. An especially prevalent story blamed Hirter for deserting his post to drink a cup of tea. One grieving father even attempted to kill him. A throng of about five hundred angry people gathered in front of his home. For many days, either police or neighbors had been stationed with guns on the janitor's porch to protect Hirter from violence. A later investigation exonerated him from any negligence. He continued working as a janitor in various schools until his retirement at age seventy. Hirter died at the age of ninety-six.

Parents also blamed the school architects, incorrectly claiming they had designed the building with the outer doors opening inward. Another fable placed the fire's cause on several girls who deliberately created the blaze. A valid criticism claimed that the school's 350-pupil enrollment substantially exceeded the intended number of students for the building's design. Officially, the narrow wood stairs and obstructions of clear pathways to exits generated condemnation.

Investigators never determined the cause of the fire, but the most common belief is that an overheated furnace ignited dry wood in the boiler room.

Shortly after the fire, Cleveland annexed Collinwood, partly due to the village's inability to guarantee fire safety resources. A memorial garden eventually occupied the former school site. Cleveland constructed Collinwood Memorial, a new school, next to the garden; it remained in use into the 1970s. Following its demolition in 2004, the city built a second "Memorial" school on the same site. Nationally, the tragedy led to improved building designs, including iron staircases, concrete floors, fireproof coverings for pipes, more staircases and doors placed directly in front of the staircases.

10

Slovenian War Survivors

The Path to Cleveland

During World War II, portions of Yugoslavia's Slovenian territory endured annexations by Nazi Germany, Fascist Italy and Hungary. The Slovene Partisans, led in part by revolutionary communists, evolved into an important anti-Nazi resistance movement. Part of this faction envisioned an eventual Slovene state within a socialist Yugoslav federation. The Partisans merged with Josip Tito's communist forces in 1944.

Meanwhile, the Home Guard, opponents of the Partisans, consisted of anti-communist Slovenians. Although far more complicated in reality, Slovenians appeared to divide themselves into two groups: anti-communist (which, during the war, appeared to imply pro-Nazi) and anti-Nazi (seemingly pro-communist by default). The war thus created yet another substantial divide between two Slovenian groups. In fact, Slovenia entered into its own internal civil war during the last three years of World War II.

The complex and chaotic conditions occurring in Slovenia during the war can be partially illustrated by the saga of Metod M. Milac. Members of an Italian occupation army, located in Slovenia, first detained Milac and then forced him onto a train bound for a concentration camp in Italy. Rescued by Partisans when they attacked the train, Milac, under intimidation, volunteered to perform labor tasks. Two months later, a militant fascist Italian group recaptured him and sent him to a concentration camp, where he received barely enough food to avoid starvation. Eventually released by the Italians, the weakened Milac needed assistance to climb the ladder of the boat that would transport him to freedom.

German soldiers capture Yugoslavian citizens during World War II. *Courtesy of Cleveland Public Library, Photograph Collection.*

Next, the German Gestapo arrested Milac, sending him to Auschwitz. He escaped from German control during an evacuation march to another camp. But the Germans recaptured Milac and assigned him to work in a hospital, where he initiated yet another escape. Arresting Milac a third time, the Germans assigned him to manual labor. With the help of relatives, he escaped again. Following a long and arduous journey, he returned to

Slovenia. There the government attempted to draft him into the army but relented upon reviewing his rather incredible previous military engagements.

Observing the chaos in Slovenia and anticipating a communist takeover, Milac traveled to an Allied-controlled Austrian refugee camp. Immigrating to the United States, he earned a baccalaureate degree and a master's degree from the Cleveland Institute of Music and a master's degree in library science from Western Reserve University. He founded and directed Koroian, a group of Cleveland Slovenian immigrants who sang old folk songs. Milac relocated to Syracuse, where he received a PhD from Syracuse University. He worked at the university from 1962 until his retirement in 1992.

As World War II ended, many military and civilian Slovenian refugees duplicated Milac's journey by pouring into Austria, placing their fate in the hands of the British. Claiming to be transporting anti-communist refugees to a better camp in Italy, the British actually sent military members and their families (a total of about twelve thousand people) back to Yugoslavia to face execution. Similar relocations and deaths awaited civilian refugees considered political enemies of communist Yugoslavia.

The tormented journey of Home Guard soldiers exiled in Austria ended in Yugoslavia. Following a final round of beating and torture, communists shot Slovenian soldiers in the back at the edge of a large pit already filled with decaying corpses. France Dejak and Milan Zajec, both of whom later immigrated to Cleveland, each evaded a fatal bullet. Dejak, shot in the left thigh, fell into the abyss; Zajec jumped in before being shot. To remain alive, the two would need to avoid being crushed by new rounds of falling bodies, dodge grenades and machine-gun bullets fired at random into the pit, escape from the fifty-foot hole, avoid being seen by Partisans milling around and locate food and water. Despite nearly impossible odds, the two successfully completed all of these tasks.

To keep warm in the pit, Zajec and Dejak removed clothing from dead bodies and placed the garments on themselves. When the communists detonated explosives, sending rocks and dust into the mass grave, an uprooted tree saved their lives. Along with a few other men still alive, Zajec and Dejak climbed the tree to its top and swung themselves to the edge to obtain their freedom from the crater. Zajec had spent five days and nights, without food or water, in the deadly crevice. Splitting up, the two eventually discovered friendly villages where they received food, water and rest. Each reunited with relatives and escaped into Italy.

After immigrating to Cleveland, Dejak worked as a machinist. He died in 2013; the funeral took place at St. Mary Church in Collinwood. As a

Clevelander, Zajec became president of the American Slovenian Anti-Communist War Veterans Association.

Max Rak, another Home Guard solider being transported from Austria back to Slovenia to face death, noticed that his uniform matched that of the Partisans except for the inclusion of a red star. He used a pair of appropriated scissors to cut a red section from a Slovenia flag and shaped it into a star. While hiding in a bathroom, he attached the phony star to his uniform. After barking bogus orders at a few Partisan soldiers, Rak saluted the guards, walked out of his captivity and eventually immigrated to Cleveland, where he became a successful doctor.

Uros Roessmann enrolled in the Ljubljana University Medical School program in 1943, but the school closed within a few weeks of his entrance. The next year, he joined the Home Guard after receiving assurance that he would be used as a medic. In 1945, after ending up in an Austrian refugee camp, he understood that he must escape to avoid death. In a daring move, he discarded his uniform, changed into a suit and transferred himself to a civilian camp. He immigrated to Cleveland, settling on East Sixty-Eighth Street near St. Clair Avenue. In 1957, he earned a doctorate in medicine from Western Reserve University and married Milci Lekan, the sister of Home Guard fighter Joze Lekan. The ceremony took place at St. Vitus Church. Roessmann, still living in Cleveland, became an expert in neuropathology.

Matej Roesessmann, the brother of Uros, also joined the Home Guard, transferred to a civilian refugee camp and immigrated to Cleveland. A wealthy sponsor family employed Matej and his wife, Pepca, as domestic help and assisted him in obtaining a law degree from the Western Reserve University Law School. Matej had already earned a law degree in Slovenia, but it was not recognized in the United States.

Just prior to the last evacuation of military refugees, Austrian refugee camp officials learned positively what had been rumored for months: previous military refugees transported from the camp had all been killed. The officials advised a few remaining military refugees that they could remain at the camp as civilians. But a few, as a show of respect and solidarity to their former friends, chose to return to Slovenia to face death. Joseph "Joze" Lekan, who had joined the Home Guard as a teenager, elected to go back to Slovenia. His father (the director of utilities in the city of Maribor) intervened, demanding that Joze remain in the camp. The action most likely saved his son's life.

Dr. Valentin Mersol had spent five years in a Russian prison camp during World War I. Following the war, he earned a medical degree from the University of Prague and later studied at Johns Hopkins University.

In 1985, Slovenians gathered at St. John Cathedral to participate in a memorial service honoring the fortieth anniversary of the massacre of thousands of Slovenians by the communist regime in Yugoslavia. *Courtesy of Cleveland Public Library, Photograph Collection.*

Returning to Yugoslavia, Dr. Mersol became the personal physician to Yugoslav King Alexander and the royal family. He married a woman possessing a doctorate degree and fluency in six languages. During World War II, Mersol treated Home Guard soldiers by concealing them in an infectious disease section, reasoning that Germans would not risk acquiring a disease by searching the area. The anti-communist doctor and his family then fled on foot across the Alps to Austria.

Refugee camp members chose Dr. Mersol to represent them as spokesman to the British. He intervened in the Slovenian relocation crisis. Although too late to save the soldiers and their families, he helped obtain an agreement with British authorities to stop further deportation to Slovenia and to guarantee that Yugoslavians would not be forced to return to their homeland against their will. The agreement took effect just twelve hours before the first group of Slovenian civilians (numbering about twenty-seven hundred) would have been sent back to their mother country to die. His efforts assisted in saving the lives of thousands of additional exiled persons who would have been killed had they returned to Yugoslavia.

After his political victory, a car accident caused severe injury to Dr. Mersol. At the same time, his wife endured cancer treatment. In 1949, the Mersol family immigrated to Cleveland, where he established a medical practice on St. Clair Avenue. Five years after his 1975 retirement, Dr. Mersol died just prior to his eighty-eighth birthday.

Dr. Mersol's son Val, who had spent time in a refugee camp as a youth, considered the educational curriculum in the camp to be more difficult than that of Cleveland schools. Val worked in a turkey farm and milked cows to earn money to attend medical school. He developed an ear, nose and throat practice and resided in Chagrin Falls.

Eleven-year-old Frank Jeglic, whose father served as director of Slovenian Primary Education, departed with his parents to a refugee camp in Austria. After immigrating to America, he studied engineering at Notre Dame University, working as a garbage collector when he ran out of money. After earning his degree, Jeglic worked for NASA and for Babcock and Wilcox in Cleveland.

Anton Oblak lost an eye fighting with the Home Guard. Two years after the end of World War II, his father, mother and five brothers safely returned to Slovenia's farmland. Anton, in his early twenties, and his teenage sister immigrated to Cleveland, where he resided until his death in 2011 at the age of eighty-eight. During his life in Cleveland, he worked for Fisher Body, a brickyard and a machine shop.

A former St. Clair Avenue neighborhood resident, born in an Austrian refugee camp, recalled the trauma her parents endured following the war's end. Her father had fled from Slovenia with the intention of summoning the family after he reached a refugee camp. Meanwhile, a communist soldier entered their home, demanding that the escapee's wife reveal her husband's whereabouts. To demonstrate his seriousness, he held a gun to the head of the wife's less-than-one-year-old daughter. To the soldier's surprise, the infant responded by giving him a big smile. The mother truthfully explained that she did not know where her husband had fled. The soldier departed, his resistance softened by the baby's beam and his belief that the mother would not lie with her infant daughter in such peril.

With the major breadwinner of the family gone, the communist regime offered little opposition to freeing the wife and children. But many Slovenians waited years in refugee camps while securing a sponsor to make immigration to the United States possible. About one thousand Slovenian refugees, many saved from death by Dr. Mersol, settled in the St. Clair neighborhood.

11

The Slovenian Food Scene

Dining Out and Home Cooking

Slovenian immigrant Frank Sterle arrived in New York in 1956 without a cent to his name. A Catholic group had loaned him three dollars to purchase food to eat during his journey to Cleveland. Sterle's first job in the city consisted of picking apples at twenty cents per bushel; he earned ten dollars a week. Sterle soon switched to a machine shop paying thirty cents per hour. Four years later, he had accumulated enough money to purchase the twenty-seat Bonna Café, located on East Fifty-Fifth Street.

In 1973, Sterle bought the building housing his café; he also purchased nine nearby homes. Remodeling the building's exterior to resemble an Alpine hunting lodge, he created a restaurant (Frank Sterle's Country House) in the former café and added living space above the eatery to house his wife, Ann, and himself. Demolition of the homes that he had acquired produced space for a convenient parking lot next to his new restaurant venture.

In 1986, Sterle died of heart failure in his home above the Country House. To accommodate the large crowds at his wake, his body rested on the stage at the St. Clair Slovenian National Home.

Italian immigrant Mike Longo, a sewer contractor with no restaurant experience, purchased the restaurant. He hired Margot Glinski, a German immigrant from Nuremberg, to manage his new investment. She had been a server for fifteen years at the Hofbrau Haus, located almost directly across the street from the Country House. Initially, many Slovenians predicted a dire future for the restaurant, now owned by an Italian and managed by a German. But the restaurant's name, menu items and cooks remained mostly unchanged; Frank Sterle's Country House continued to thrive.

Above: Frank Sterle's Slovenian Country House has been a familiar East Fifty-Fifth Street restaurant since 1973. *Courtesy of the author.*

Left: Striking murals reminiscent of Slovenia embellish the interior of Sterle's Restaurant. *Courtesy of Special Collections, Michael Schwartz Library, Cleveland State University.*

Following the death of Longo, Rick Semersky purchased the eatery. Inspired by his motto, "Honor the past and ensure the future," Semersky added new menu items and entertainment offerings while never deviating from the Slovenian food and polka evenings that had made the restaurant a landmark. Visitors to the Country House still admired large, hand-painted murals depicting people, snow-covered mountains, lakes, forests, stone castles and other scenes reminiscent of Slovenia. Patrons eagerly consume stuffed cabbage, meatloaf, stroganoff, pork chops, roast veal and Wiener schnitzel while polka bands entertain on weekends. In 2017, the restaurant closed to the public but remained in existence as a private event center.

Martin Sorn immigrated to Cleveland in 1905 and, in 1917, established Sorn's Restaurant on St. Clair Avenue. From an initial twenty-eight chairs surrounding seven tables, the eatery expanded to accommodate one hundred diners. Through the decades, customers included factory and office workers,

In 1967, Sorn's St. Clair Avenue Restaurant celebrated its fiftieth anniversary. *Courtesy of the Plain Dealer.*

politicians, entertainers performing at the nearby Slovenian Home and Cleveland Browns players following their practices at League Park. A 1963 dinner special featured prime rib, baked potato and salad for two dollars and fifty cents.

Martin and his immigrant wife, Caroline, lived above the restaurant with their family. Following forty-six years of marriage, she died in 1952. When Martin died in 1967, his son and daughter operated the restaurant into 1970.

For thirty-eight years, Louis Erste operated a winery in his home on Schade Avenue near the intersection of Superior Avenue and East Sixty-Fifth Street. He also established a retail wine shop on St. Clair Avenue. After Louis's death in 1957, his daughter Bertha Lobe converted the wine store into the Slovenian Village restaurant. Bertha's husband, Slovenian-born Henry Lobe, had earned a doctor of law degree from Ljubljana University in 1940. During World War II, he escaped from a prison camp by crossing the Austrian Alps on skis.

Requiring more space, Bertha later relocated the restaurant four blocks to the east. In either location, Slovenian Village patrons always enjoyed fresh food. When Bertha ran out of meat or produce, she simply embarked on a very short journey to a nearby butcher shop or grocery store to replenish her supply. In 1963, home-cooked breaded veal a la Ljubljana (including potatoes, salad and bread) cost two dollars and twenty-five cents, the most expensive item on the menu. Tripe stew and Slovenian goulash with dumplings constituted two other customer favorites.

In North Collinwood, three generations of Slovenians patronized Fanny's Restaurant on East 156th Street, a few blocks north of Waterloo Road. In 1947, Frances Boldin and her daughter Frances Kollar opened the ethnic eatery serving Slovenian sausage, pork risotto and pork-kraut goulash as featured items. Fourteen years later, to accommodate a growing clientele, Fanny's relocated into a former farmhouse about two blocks down the street.

Three of Frances Kollar's children (Terry, Bert and Shirley Davido) continued as third-generation operators of the restaurant. As the years progressed, Fanny's added a variety of hamburger choices to the menu while still offering traditional ethnic dishes. An online reviewer commented, "the food is just like Mom used to make for Sunday dinners." Another reviewer verified that the restaurant never quite resembled a trendy eatery: "It looks like it was decorated by the grandmother." Business declined as East 156th Street turned into a haven for drug dealers. The restaurant finally closed in 2007, just short of its sixtieth anniversary.

In addition to restaurant dining, Cleveland Slovenians have enhanced their own cooking experience by purchasing food from a variety of local stores and butcher shops. Sausage, ranking high on the list of Slovenian favorites, can be purchased in virtually any conventional grocery store. Yet customers regularly travel fifty miles or more to obtain authentic Slovenian sausage at St. Clair Avenue and Collinwood butcher shops.

The unique taste created by each store is achieved by preparing and seasoning quality meats using spices and condiments such as salt, garlic, pepper, paprika, nutmeg, ginger and caraway. Fillers, including rice, add to the taste. The flavor of smoked sausage is further defined by the wood (or sawdust) used and the length of the cooking process. One Cleveland sausage maker guarded his secret recipe by coding each ingredient with a number, rather than identifying it by name, and then locking the formula in a safe-deposit box.

For Frank Azman, a third-generation sausage maker on St. Clair Avenue, crafting smoked sausage is a meticulous five- or six-day undertaking. First, fat is removed from the meat, which is then cut into smaller pieces and ground. A garlic paste, created in a food processor, is added to the meat, along with spices. Garlic soaked in water also enhances the meat's flavor. A

In his St. Clair Avenue smokehouse, Frank Azman displays a batch of his famous sausages. *Courtesy of the author.*

William and Frank Azman (*left*) demonstrate the initial meat-cutting stage of sausage making while their brothers Louis and Edward (*right*) display the final product. *Courtesy of Frank Azman.*

sausage stuffer is used to place the meat in the casings. The sausage is then twisted into the desired size and hung on a sausage stick. As part of the curing procedure, the sausage is placed in a cooler. The meat is then taken to a backyard smokehouse, where it is simultaneously cooked and smoked, using cherry wood, for about one hour.

The Azman sausage shop debuted in 1917. After working in a Detroit Ford Motor plant for five dollars a day, founder Frank Azman established his combined grocery store and meat market that has developed into a neighborhood institution. Now entering its second century, the success of Frank's business might have been predicted; decades earlier, his father had founded a sausage business in Slovenia.

Frank, along with his wife, four sons and two daughters, lived in an apartment in the back of the store. The children worked in the business from an early age, stocking shelves, cleaning floors, packing groceries and learning the specifics of running a successful meat market. In 1955, Frank turned the daily store operations over to his four sons (Louis, William, Edward and Frank Jr.). He died the following year at the age of seventy-one, but the family business continued to prosper.

In 1959, the brothers purchased a 1926 Model T Ford to promote the store at local festivals and parades. Louis, accompanied by his wife, usually drove the antique automobile. The couple wore vintage 1920s costumes to attract attention to themselves and to their market.

Frank Jr. greeted loyal customers, some residing as far away as Lorain and Chardon, by their first names. Making them seem part of an extended family, he inquired about their health and the activities of their children. But time eventually took its toll on the four brothers. An illness forced Edward into retirement. In 1993, Louis, who had worked his entire life in the business, collapsed in the store and died from a heart attack at the age of eighty-two. Frank died in 2004; William followed in 2010 at the age of ninety-six. Frank (the grandson of the founder and son of Frank Jr.) now operates the store. The legendary Slovenian sausage is still smoked in a brick smokehouse located at the back of the store.

Meanwhile, William's son William Jr. founded Azman Quality Meats on East 185th Street in Collinwood, later moving the business eastward to East 200th Street in Euclid. In addition to loyal local customers, both Azman stores have shipped their homemade sausages to various parts of the world and, in one instance, even beyond. An astronaut born in Euclid, Ohio, requested that a shipment of Cleveland Slovenian sausages from William's store be sent to the International Space Station, where she could enjoy the unique food while in outer space.

Frank (grandson of the original owner) stands outside the St. Clair Avenue shop where his grandfather, father and uncles had previously carried on the business. *Courtesy of the author.*

At the age of eighteen, Slovenian immigrant Rudy Bukovec worked in an East Forty-Ninth Street meat market where he mastered the meat-cutting trade. Ten years later, in 1928, Rudy established his own butcher shop on Superior Avenue near East Forty-Fifth Street. His wife, Agnes, took over the business when Rudy died in a 1937 automobile accident. In 1955, she opened a second store at East Sixty-Seventh Street and St. Clair Avenue. Eight years later, a third store debuted in Willowick, Ohio. Following Agnes's death in 1960, her three sons continued the suburban store but closed the two Cleveland locations.

Joe Zuzak prepared himself for his food career by studying for three years in a Slovenian chef school. Today, he owns the R&D Sausage Shop located on Waterloo Road in Collinwood. In addition to sausage, he prepares stuffed cabbage, stuffed peppers and strudel.

In 1927, Ludwig Raddell opened a Collinwood sausage shop that has continued to prosper for more than four generations. Today, about one thousand pounds of Slovenian smoked sausage are carefully crafted each week for sale at the East 152nd Street store. Potica lovers also make regular trips to the store, where Slovenian cookbooks and Raddell T-shirts are also available.

Slovenians have journeyed to ethnic events in Kirtland, Ohio (located about nineteen miles east of Cleveland), since 1938, when the Slovene National Benefit Society purchased a farm in the town. Every fall since 2004, hundreds of sausage lovers have traveled to Kirtland to attend the annual Slovenian Sausage Festival, which includes a "King of Klobasa" contest. As multiple polka bands perform, judges select the best of the year's entries. Originating in Slovenia, some of the sausage recipes have been passed down from immigrants for more than a century. The winner hangs a banner at his or her store and obtains an exclusive contract for sausage vending at Cleveland's annual downtown Thanksgiving Polka Festival.

Similar to the sausage contests, the Collinwood Slovenian Workman's Home in 1985 launched a bakeoff competition. About seventy-five to one hundred bakers entered their cooking into one or more of five categories representing traditional Slovenian baked goods: flancate (angel wings), potica (nut, raisin and tarragon rolls), krofe (raised doughnuts), strudel (apple, cherry, apricot and cheese) and bread. The thirty-piece United Slovenian Band and Joey Tomsick's orchestra provided listening and dancing entertainment at the original bakeoff.

The creation of delicious Slovenian baked goods involves an art form as well as a recipe. The crafting of strudel with hand-pulled dough, for example, requires that the dough be carefully stretched over a cloth-covered table. The dough must be prepared as thin as paper but not torn. During the initial stretching process, when the dough is still thick, the backs of the fingers are used. As the dough thins by being spread across the table, the baker shifts to using the fingertips to continue the stretching. Fruit is then distributed evenly near one edge of the stretched dough. One hem of the tablecloth is lifted so that the dough curls over the fruit. As the tablecloth is raised higher, the dough rolls over itself. If executed correctly, a narrow roll about six feet long is created just as the strudel reaches the other side of the table. The rolled-up strudel is then ready to be baked, with the hand-pulled dough forming the strudel's tasty crust.

The legacy of Slovenian cooking continues as new generations learn from their parents or enroll in cooking classes at neighborhood community centers or churches. Classes in baked-goods cooking are a specialty provided at St. Mary Church in Collinwood.

12

Slovenian Politics

Personalities, Parties and Issues

Only two people's political careers have encompassed serving as mayor of Cleveland, governor of Ohio and member of the United States Senate. Both politicians grew up in a Cleveland Slovenian neighborhood: Frank J. Lausche (born and raised on St. Clair Avenue) and George Voinovich (a native of Collinwood). Each success lifted the spirits of the hometown community and inspired other Slovenians to pursue political careers.

Slovenian immigrants Frances and Louis Lausche settled in Cleveland in the mid-1880s. On November 14, 1894, Frances gave birth to Frank J. Lausche in her St. Clair Avenue home. Louis worked in a steel mill at the time and later thrived in real estate and as a wine merchant operating a St. Clair Avenue store. But he died in 1908 with Frances expecting their tenth child.

Frank attended St. Vitus Grade School and Central High School. To help support the large family, he also worked as a lamplighter and sold newspapers. When his father died, Frank dropped out of high school to help his widowed mother operate a restaurant. He later attended night school to obtain his high school diploma.

A dangerous hitter and excellent third baseman in Cleveland's Slovenian softball leagues, Lausche also excelled in minor league baseball. In 1914, he is credited with setting a world's record by registering fourteen assists and a putout in a single game. He joined the army in 1918 and served as a second lieutenant. Following World War I, Lausche turned down a professional baseball contract to attend Cleveland's John Marshall Law

School. He scored second-highest on the state bar exam and established a successful law practice.

In 1922, Lausche entered the political arena, quickly displaying the somewhat unorthodox style that would define his career in politics. Battling for a seat in the Ohio House of Representatives, the twenty-seven-year-old lawyer campaigned in Chagrin Falls, one of northeast Ohio's happily driest locations during Prohibition. Following a superb speech and a great ovation from the local crowd, he responded to a question about Prohibition by calling the alcohol ban a bad law, adding, "Right now, I would like a cold beer." He received only four votes from the residents of Chagrin Falls in his losing cause. Two years later, he failed again in his bid for an Ohio house seat.

In 1928, Lausche married Jane Sheal, an interior decorator and graduate of the Cleveland School of Art. Jane learned to speak Slovenian while washing the dinner dishes; she pinned lists of Slovenian words and their translations above her kitchen sink, memorizing them during the dishwashing chore. A valuable partner for her husband when he returned to politics, she often dined with city hall reporters and accompanied them to city council meetings. Jane also had a remarkable knack for remembering people's names. In 1941, a minor officeholder congratulated her on her husband's mayoral victory. Before he could introduce himself, she called him by name and even recalled their only previous meeting, an event at the Glenville Methodist Church.

Back in politics in 1931, Lausche took over a Democratic ward leadership. The following year, Ohio's governor, George White, appointed him a municipal judge. Two years later, voters elected Lausche to a four-year term. In 1935, he won a six-year term as a common pleas judge, the only Slovenian in the United States to occupy a judgeship of that rank in the common pleas court. He also reigned as the second-youngest judge on the common pleas bench in the United States.

In 1940, the *Plain Dealer* identified Lausche as a rising star in Cleveland politics. The next year, he won the first of his two Cleveland mayoral terms by securing 71 percent of the vote. Lausche became the city's first mayor of eastern European descent.

Following his mayoral success, Lausche served five terms as Ohio's governor, the first Catholic to hold that office. In 1944, he spent $27,132 to win his first governorship; James Garfield Stewart, his opponent, expended $800,000 in a losing effort. In the late afternoon of Election Day, as return coverage began on radio, Lausche amused himself on a golf course. In

Jubilant supporters surround Frank Lausche, winner of the 1941 Cleveland mayoral election. *Courtesy of Cleveland Public Library, Photograph Collection.*

1946, Clevelander Thomas J. Herbert narrowly defeated Lausche in the Slovenian's bid for reelection. Two years later, he regained the governorship, which he kept for three more terms. Lausche concluded his political career with two terms in the U.S. Senate.

During his memorable career, he obtained a well-deserved reputation for wearing rumpled clothes and off-center ties. He taunted reporters and political writers, sometimes answering their questions in Slovenian. He endorsed Republican candidates in state elections and supported Ohio Republican Robert A. Taft in his bid to become U.S. president. Lausche twice endorsed Richard Nixon for president. Both Democrat Harry Truman and Republican Dwight Eisenhower considered Lausche as a possible running mate. As a Democrat, he turned into a nemesis of organized labor by failing to support increased government spending. The loss of labor union support finally ended his political career, although he remained in Bethesda, Maryland, in private practice. Gravely ill in 1990, at the age of ninety-four, he returned to Cleveland to spend his final days.

Frank Lausche used this postcard to promote his successful campaign to regain the governorship of Ohio. *Courtesy of the author.*

Born in 1936 to immigrant parents (a Slovenian mother and a Serbian father), George Voinovich's Slovenian roots traversed many generations: his great-grandfather played an organ in a Ljubljana church. Voinovich contracted a childhood bone-marrow disease that limited his ability to run. He compensated for his predicament by learning to ride a red bicycle that he named Bessie. Prior to graduating from Collinwood High School in 1954, he had acted in the Collinwood Players production of *Life with Father*. He earned a degree in government from Ohio University (1958) and a law degree from the Ohio State College of Law (1961).

Voinovich met Lakewood resident Janet Allan at a 1960 Cleveland Republican event; George diligently worked inflating balloons while an equally attentive Janet served cookies. The couple married following his graduation from law school. Quiet, shy and uninterested in the public spotlight, Janet even devised a plan to avoid a public speaking class while in high school.

Voinovich launched his political career as an assistant attorney general of Ohio. In 1966, he won an election to the Ohio House of Representatives, even though his only newspaper endorsement came from the *Collinwood Press*.

By 1968, Cleveland Republican leaders had taken notice of the "aggressive young state representative from Collinwood," considering him as a possible candidate to oppose the reelection of Carl Stokes. Three years later, Voinovich unsuccessfully entered a Cleveland mayoral contest, losing to county auditor Ralph J. Perk in the primary election. This would be the first of only two elections that he would ever lose. When Perk became mayor, he selected Voinovich to replace him as auditor. In the next election, voters chose Voinovich to continue in that position.

In 1963, while George served as county auditor, he and Janet purchased a home in Collinwood for $16,500. He lived in it for the rest of his life (fifty-four years) except for his time in the governor's mansion. Following a two-year stint as county commissioner, Voinovich rose to the position of lieutenant governor in the James Rhodes administration. Totally befuddling his political advisors and experts, he resigned his key state position after less than one year to oppose Dennis Kucinich as Cleveland's mayor. At the time, fiscal problems and a near-deserted downtown characterized one of the lowest periods in the city's history. Panhandlers even entered George's downtown campaign headquarters on East Fourteenth Street, promising to vote for him in exchange for ten dollars or free cookies or doughnuts. On a tragic personal level, his nine-year-old daughter Molly died from injuries suffered after being hit by a driver who had crashed into a traffic light on Lake Shore Boulevard.

Supported by some labor unions, Voinovich won the 1979 mayoral election by gathering 56 percent of the votes, including a majority from African Americans. In 1981, a remarkable 76 percent reelected him to Cleveland's first four-year mayoral term. In the next election (1985), he won by attracting 72 percent of the vote.

In 1988, while still governing Cleveland, Voinovich lost an election for his second and final time; Howard Metzenbaum defeated him in a U.S. Senate race. In his political lifetime, Voinovich won twenty-eight of his thirty election bids.

In 1990, 56 percent of the Ohio electorate chose to send Voinovich to the governor's mansion in Columbus. In 1994, 72 percent reelected him. Ohio voters then sent Voinovich to the U.S. Senate, where he acted as a leading voice on the turmoil in the Balkan countries. With 64 percent of the votes, he easily won his 2004 reelection bid. In fact, every one of Ohio's eighty-eight counties supplied Voinovich with a majority of the votes. Voinovich demonstrated independence similar to that of Frank Lausche by not supporting George Bush on several issues, including the No Child Left Behind Act. The senator explained, "The United States and Congress are not the school board of the United States."

Meanwhile, as a dutiful politician's wife, Janet volunteered at healthcare facilities. During her eighteen years in the public spotlight (ten years as Cleveland's First Lady and eight more as the state's First Lady), she learned to be comfortable delivering speeches during George's campaigns, at times even denouncing what she considered unfair political attacks on her husband. As the governor's wife, she served as a spokesperson for her own causes, such as breast cancer awareness, education and child health issues.

Promoting fiscal responsibility throughout his political career, Voinovich demonstrated the same frugality in his personal life. In 1969, he spent a total of sixty-nine cents to attend one of Richard Nixon's inaugural balls. After receiving a free ticket and transportation from a friend, he packed one of his black suits and paid sixty-nine cents for a bow tie. He continued his unassuming lifestyle throughout his life. In 1991, Voinovich received a lifetime achievement award from the Kiwi Shoe Polish Company, a prize for his insistence on shining his own shoes.

Janet proved to be George's equal in thriftiness. An accomplished seamstress, she made her own gowns for her husband's three mayoral galas. During Ronald Reagan's 1981 inaugural ball at the Kennedy Center, Janet wore a tapestry dress she had sewn five years earlier. For President Reagan's 1985 inauguration, Janet wore a burgundy taffeta she had made herself. At her husband's gubernatorial swearing-in ceremony, she created her own porcelain white, wool, crepe chemise suit.

While visiting Washington in 1991, Janet proudly purchased a new $50.00 jumpsuit marked down in price to $15.99. When George lost his gloves, Janet bought him a new pair but paid much more that she desired. A Cleveland Uncle Bill's discount store, her usual outlet for purchasing gloves, sold merchandise for considerably less money.

As Ohio's First Lady, Janet converted the governor's former meditation space into a sewing room. She redecorated the mansion with tasteful 1920s-era furniture and bric-a-brac often obtained at flea markets and estate sales.

George Voinovich retired from politics in 2010; six years later, he unexpectedly died in his sleep, only four weeks before his eightieth birthday. In his final public appearance, less than forty-eighty hours prior to his death, he commemorated Slovenian Independence Day in an address at Cleveland City Hall.

During the nearly nine decades spanning the combined careers of Frank Lausche and George Voinovich, members of Cleveland's Slovenian neighborhoods demonstrated a keen interest in politics. By 1916, the Slovenian American Political Club of Cleveland (headquartered on St. Clair Avenue) had recruited about eight hundred members.

Beginning about 1910, early socialist political parties conducted largely unsuccessful recruitment meetings at various Slovenian meeting places on St. Clair Avenue. In 1927, the St. Clair Slovenian Home held a memorial service for Cleveland-born socialist Charles Emil Ruthenberg, a longtime head of the Communist Party USA. Prior to his ascent into national Communist leadership, Ruthenberg had run unsuccessfully for political positions eight times in one decade: mayor of Cleveland (1911, 1915, 1917 and 1919), governor of Ohio (1912), U.S. senator (1914) and member of the U.S. House of Representatives (1916 and 1918).

During the Depression, the Slovenian National Home on St. Clair Avenue hosted numerous left-wing speakers. National Socialist Party leader Norman Thomas, who ran for president in 1928, called for unemployment payments of twenty-five dollars per week. Similarly, William Z. Foster, a candidate for the presidency on the Communist Party ticket, asked for support to implement unemployment insurance.

Frank Crosswaith, editor of the *Negro Labor News*, told St. Clair residents, "The present depression is due to the close relationship of industry and politics." He continued, "The masters of trades are not concertedly attempting to end the depression. The end will come only when the masses of workers show their strength at the polls and take over the reins of government by intelligent voting."

In 1931, one thousand communist sympathizers at the St. Clair Slovenian Home commemorated the seventh anniversary of Nikolai Lenin's death. I.O. Ford, the primary speaker and recent candidate for Ohio governor on the Communist Workers' Party ticket, stood beneath a banner proclaiming "Defend the Soviet Union, the Worker's Fatherhood." On the same program, R. Shohan, a member of the Young Communist League, told the crowd that revolutionary workers were penetrating the army, the National Guard, war industries and the YMCA, so that "when the time comes, we will know how to turn the bosses' guns against them."

After attending a 1931 communist meeting, about three hundred people gathered at East Forty-Seventh Street near Woodland Avenue to protest the eviction of a person from his home. A few of the demonstrators attacked law enforcement officers present at the gathering. In retaliation, the police shot and killed two of the protestors. A jury ruled that the shootings constituted justifiable self-defense.

The incident inspired a communist-staged mock trial conducted at the St. Clair Slovenian Home. About fourteen hundred persons paid fifteen cents each to witness the event. The "defendants" included the government of Cleveland, various newspapers, the American Federation of Labor and the Socialist Party. William Z. Foster, a national secretary of the Trade Union Unity League and three-time Communist Party candidate for president, acted as the prosecutor. No one represented the defense. An all-communist jury found every defendant guilty and imposed its sentence: the overthrow of the government and its replacement by a new communist regime.

In 1933, a local committee of the Continental Congress of Workers and Farmers, one of the most radical political groups in existence during the Great Depression, organized a local committee during a St. Clair Avenue conference. Following World War II, the St. Clair Independent Socialists League of Cleveland organized to oppose both American capitalism and Russian communism.

The St. Clair neighborhood also demonstrated its anti-communist outlook. In 1950, two hundred pickets (not all Slovenians) jammed the front of the St. Clair Slovenian National Home to protest a meeting of the communist-supported Lithuanian Literary Association. As members of the association entered the hall, pickets pelted them with eggs. After milling around for about two hours, the pickets surged into the meeting room, interrupted the gathering and staged their own demonstrations.

Cleveland supporters of Tito's regime in Yugoslavia sponsored a dinner in 1954 to honor Vladimir Popovic, the Yugoslavian ambassador to the United States. Prior to the dinner, a line of sixty-five Slovenian and Croatian pickets greeted the ambassador as he entered Collinwood's Slovenian Workman's Home. Earlier in the day, seven Yugoslavs had burst into Popovic's hotel room to "ask some questions." The incident ended without serious problems.

Radicals did not sponsor all of the political gatherings in Slovenian neighborhoods. Throughout the decades, mainstream Republican and Democratic candidates held numerous peaceful rallies and meetings at many of the Cleveland Slovenian Homes. Edward M. Kennedy, running for president in 1978, appeared at the St. Clair hall. In 1980, while Democrats held a fundraiser—$2,500.00 per couple—for Jimmy Carter in Shaker Heights, the Cuyahoga County Republicans used the St. Clair Avenue Slovenian Home to stage a $0.98 chicken dinner comprising two pieces of chicken, coleslaw, bread, butter and a beverage. The local Republican Party chairman commented to the audience of about one thousand, "Unlike President Carter, we're trying to hold the line on inflation." Bob Dole campaigned for president on St. Clair Avenue in 1995, as did John Kerry in 2004. George Voinovich used the Holmes Avenue Slovenian Home as a base for many of his political campaigns.

In 1925, Slovenian-born John L. Mihelich became the first Slovenian in the United States to be elected to a city council position. Mihelich had settled in the St. Clair Avenue neighborhood in 1907, working for the Gund brewery. Ten years later, he served as Cleveland's first Slovenian lawyer.

Joseph W. Kovach, a Slovenian resident of East Eighty-Second Street in Newburgh, served as a city councilman and a Democratic state representative for four years. In his tenure as a state representative during World War II, he introduced a bill to permit members of the armed forces to cross toll bridges without charge. He also sponsored legislation to make Good Friday a legal holiday.

During the mayoral administration of Dennis Kucinich, Betty and Tonia Grdina (granddaughters of Slovenian community leader Anton Grdina) ranked among the city's most contentious employees. Intelligent, hardworking, frugal with taxpayers' money and passionately concerned about eliminating government corruption, the sisters nevertheless created considerable controversy during their short periods of public employment in Cleveland. In a *Plain Dealer* story, a city politician characterized the sisters as "a team of young, arrogant, know-nothings who are busy insulting everybody." Another city hall employee commented, "They are people who do not know how to be polite. They don't know simple courtesies, only threats." A *Plain Dealer* editorial supporting the recall of Mayor Kucinich stated that the two sisters had been "abusive and arrogant to city employees and the public at large."

In 1977, Cleveland mayor-elect Dennis Kucinich announced his forthcoming appointment of Tonia Grdina, then a twenty-one-year-old college student two years into a degree in sociology at Cleveland State University, to the position of secretary of police. Kucinich changed her title from secretary to the safety director when he learned that the original position would have violated a state law requiring a civil service examination. A year later, she received a promotion to assistant safety director despite her lack of police or firefighting experience. In fact, Tonia's most-mentioned past experience centered on her employment in a fast-food restaurant. Kucinich offered Tonia the position of acting police chief while the official chief took a few days off to get married. She turned down the job when a reporter noted that the appointment would have violated a provision in the city charter.

William J. McNea, president of the Cleveland Police Patrolmen's Association, claimed that contract negotiations between the city and the police proved difficult because of the inexperience of the city negotiators, "including the one still wearing her training bra." McNea also referred to Tonia as "a former McDonald flipper." She countered by refusing to dispatch snowplows to clear West Fifty-Eighth Street in front of the Police Patrolmen's Hall. Shortly after Tonia's departure when Kucinich left office, police towed her car from Chester Avenue near East Twenty-Fourth Street because of a rush-hour parking violation.

Tonia married Terry Hinkle, Kucinich's utilities director. The two relocated to Cody, Wyoming, where Terry became a long-term precinct committeeman. The pair still oppose and quarrel with local Republicans, especially those affiliated with the Tea Party movement.

Betty Grdina earned a degree from Case Western Reserve University with a double major in sociology and political science. When she was twenty-two years old, Kucinich appointed her assistant director of community development. Within a short time, she was named the director of community development. Betty created many confrontations with neighborhood groups when she refused federal grant money for development projects. The St. Clair–Superior Coalition marched along East Sixth Street, between the city's community development center and city hall, protesting the rejection of a federal housing program. The parade's highlight featured an inflatable bunny and a basket filled with 147 jellybeans, one for each vacant house in the neighborhood. The coalition left an Easter basket for Betty filled with a cardboard model of a vacant house and pieces of debris from a real home.

In a letter to Cleveland officials, the Department of Housing and Urban Development (HUD) stated that the city faced a reduction in grants. The letter criticized the handling of neighborhood improvement funds and noted "employees in Ms. Grdina's department are either incompetent or unqualified and appear to be hampered by political pressures." Betty later graduated from law school and became a lawyer for the United Auto Workers Union and the Teamsters Union. She is now a Washington, D.C. lawyer specializing in labor and civil rights issues.

13

Slovenian Culture

Music, Dancing and Drama

In 1929, Mrs. Louis Sternad amused a group of St. Clair Avenue children by performing a dance while balancing a basket the size of a washtub on her head. Sternad combined her rather uncommon form of entertainment with a valuable message for the children: In Ljubljana, females carried groceries and the wash on their heads in similar-sized baskets; the balancing act represented an important part of everyday household chores.

As the Roaring Twenties ended, Mr. and Mrs. Sternad and their three children embarked on a cultural visit to Slovenia. Along with absorbing Slovenian arts, the family imported their own version of Cleveland Slovenian artistry. The Sternad Trio, comprising eighteen-year-old Josephine on accordion, sixteen-year-old Rudi playing the banjo and fourteen-year-old Teresa's piano accompaniment, presented an Americanized selection of Slovenian music. Josephine's expertise with the accordion may have surprised a few Slovenians, since females rarely played the instrument in their homeland.

Through the decades, Slovenian culture has been passed down from generation to generation. Founded in 1920, the Jardan Singing Society became one of the first tenants of the Slovenian Workman's Home on Waterloo Road when the facility opened six years later. Their presentations of classic operas, all performed in the Slovenian language, included *The Barber of Seville*, *La Traviata*, *The Marriage of Figaro*, *Il Trovatore*, *Carmen*, *Mignon* and *The Tales of Hoffman*. After performing for eighty-four years, the choir disbanded in 2004.

Members of the popular Cleveland Slovenian band Bled (named after a town in Slovenia) pose for a picture in 1916. *Courtesy of Special Collections, Michael Schwartz Library, Cleveland State University.*

Perhaps Cleveland's most famous Slovenian cultural organization is Zarja, the oldest existing Slovenian choral group outside of Slovenia. Founded in 1916 by members of the Jugoslav Socialist Federation, the Zarja Singing Society began with eighteen original members. In 1928, the group staged *Turjaska Rosamunda*, its first full-length Slovenian operatic presentation. The next year, Zarja produced the American debut of *Urh, Count of Celje*, the first Slovenian opera ever written. The performance, staged at the St. Clair National Home, attracted Slovenians from Cleveland, nearby suburbs, Lorain, Elyria, Youngstown and Akron, along with an entire Slovenian singing group from Detroit. In 1930, the group, now composed of forty-five members, presented the Slovenian opera *The Nightingale of Gorenjska* at the downtown Public Hall Little Theater.

In 1930, Zarja split into two groups, the Socialistic Zarja and Independent Zarja (renamed Glasbena Matica in 1940). Zarja has toured Slovenia at least six times and still stages local concerts throughout the year. Glasbena Matica also remains active in presenting cultural performances in the Cleveland area.

Organist Ivan Zorman and soloist Frances Adler provide musical accompaniment during a wedding at St. Lawrence Church. Frances sewed her own hunter green dress to complement her red hat and shoes. *Courtesy of Frances "Tanny" Babic.*

John Ivanusch, a Slovenian immigrant often referred to as the "father of Slovenian opera in America," conducted Zarja from 1919 into 1931 and then the Independent Zarja for another nine years. He also headed the Jardan Singing Society and the Bled Slovenian Band, along with teaching music to hundreds of Clevelanders. Ivanusch continued living in northeast Ohio until his death in 1973 at the age of ninety-three.

Slovenian native Ivan Zorman, a poet, composer and teacher, arrived in Cleveland in 1899 at the age of fourteen. He earned degrees in language, literature and music from Western Reserve University. Zorman directed and composed music for several Slovenian singing societies, published six volumes of poetry, taught organ, piano and voice and served as the organist for St. Lawrence Church for more than forty years. Zorman remained in Cleveland until his death in 1957.

In the 1930s, a former child prodigy enhanced the reputation of Cleveland's Slovenian musical productions. Born in 1899 to a poor Slovenian family headed by a combined lumberman and stonemason, Anton Schubel presented singing concerts as a four-year-old. Before reaching the age of twenty-five, he had performed with the Slovenian National Opera in Ljubljana. In 1928, he resigned the position to present more than one hundred concerts in Slovenian communities across the United States.

Schubel immigrated to America in 1930. As a pioneering television performer, he sang Slovenian songs in his rich baritone voice during an experimental CBS broadcast in 1931. Also that year, he joined the New York Metropolitan Opera, with which he performed for fourteen years. He then worked with Carnegie Hall as a general manager and talent scout. Settling in Cleveland, Schubel directed many local singing societies ranging from Glasbena Matica to the East Ohio Gas Company Girl Chorus and the choir at St. Saua's Serbian Orthodox Church. At one point, he divided his time by spending four days each week in Cleveland and three in Washington, D.C., teaching at the Washington Institute of Music. In 1965, appreciative Slovenians gathered at the St. Clair National Home to pay Schubel a tribute for his devoted work within the local community. A few months later, he died in his studio apartment above the Slovenian Home.

The Slovenian folk dance group Folklorna Skupina Kres, formed in 1954, grew into a company of 135 performers. In 1981, dancing in authentic Slovenian costumes, the group toured Austria and Italy. Kres, still very active, performs during concerts, festivals, banquets and fairs.

The Slovenian National Homes at times have established their own cultural organizations. The St. Clair Avenue Home founded the Slovene Ivan Cankar Drama Society in 1919, even before the home itself had debuted. Augusta Danilova, a famous Slovenian stage actress, directed the company in the mid-1920s prior to her return to Slovenia. These dramas helped immigrants relive the ambiance of their "old country" and introduced the country's culture to younger, American-born Slovenians. The society staged 152 performances before disbanding in 1954.

In the first half of the twentieth century, Primoz Kogoj conducted the Prvike Drustrva Zvon Chorus. The folk music incorporated songs depicting the harvesting of fields and sewing in the home. *Courtesy of Anthony J. Trzaska.*

The dramatic organization took its name from Ivan Cankar, a left-wing Slovenian author, poet and political activist. His views had apparently aroused controversy within Cleveland's Slovenian community. Back in the mid-1930s, Ljubljana honored Cleveland with a bust of Cankar for placement in the new Yugoslavian Cultural Garden. But before the formal dedication occurred, the bust mysteriously disappeared from its storage space. The following year, fifteen thousand people attended the dedication of a replica bust, although "progressive" Slovenians boycotted the ceremony.

The St. Clair Avenue Slovenian community has also produced a nationally known magician, an Academy Award–winning artist and a rock star. John J. Grdina, the nephew of Anton Grdina, emigrated from Slovenia at the age of five and grew up on St. Clair Avenue. John developed a passionate interest in magic after accompanying his father to a performance by the famed magician Harry Keller at the Lyceum Theater on Public Square. His dad had received free passes in exchange for placing an advance show card in the window of his retail store.

More than one thousand Slovenians enjoyed each of several "Slovenian Day" outings at Cleveland's 1936 Great Lakes Exposition. *Courtesy of Cleveland Public Library, Photograph Collection.*

For two years following the Harry Keller performance, Grdina practiced in front of a mirror (his only audience) before making his public debut in one of the early St. Clair Avenue halls. The house orchestra played his introduction four times before he gained enough courage to walk onto the stage. Only married for a few weeks, his wife, Minnie, helped enhance his nerve by giving him a supportive shove into the spotlight. She later became part of the act.

The successful St. Clair show launched a twelve-year career as Grdina, along with his wife and son, traveled the country as a vaudeville act, the only professional Slovenian theater magician in the United States. He gained the friendship of the great magicians Harry Houdini and Howard Thurston, both of whom visited Grdina in his home. Houdini, while entertaining at the Cleveland Palace Theater, recognized Grdina in the audience and invited him on the stage to perform a few of his more famous tricks. Following his vaudeville career, Grdina returned to Cleveland and opened a hardware store on St. Clair Avenue.

Frank Wolcansek, born on Bonna Avenue just a block from St. Clair Avenue, attended his very first art lessons at the Slovenian National Home.

He later won an Academy Award for his artwork contributions to the 1971 animated cartoon *The Crunch Bird*.

Mark Avsec, who played keyboard for Wild Cherry tours following its two-million-selling pop hit "Play That Funky Music," grew up near the intersection of East Sixty-First Street and St. Clair Avenue. He later performed with Donnie Iris and the Cruisers and composed or co-composed much of their material, including the hit songs "Ah! Leah!" and "Love Is Like a Rock." Avsec also played with the James Gang and Mason Ruffner.

Avsec spent a considerable amount of money in defense of a frivolous lawsuit regarding one of his songs. The incident inspired him to attend the Cleveland State John Marshall College of Law, where he graduated magna cum laude. He is now a successful Cleveland attorney specializing in intellectual property law.

Slovenian's deep-seated fondness for the arts continues into the twenty-first century. In 2006, diplomat Zvone Zigon arrived in Cleveland on a four-year assignment as consul general for the Republic of Slovenia. Although his impressive resume included a doctorate in political anthropology, Zigon's most appealing trait to Cleveland Slovenians may have been his love for the country's music and his experience as a singer in prestigious touring chorale groups. Zigon totally embraced Slovenians' long-standing cultural traditions and added his own modern contribution by throwing out the first pitch at Slovenia Polka Night prior to a Lake County Captains minor league baseball contest.

14

Slovenian Polka Kings

Cleveland-Style Music

Peasants in Bohemia created the polka in the 1830s. The dance quickly spread to Prague, Paris, London and the elegant ballrooms of Vienna. By 1844, polka music had crossed the Atlantic Ocean to the United States. In Cleveland, learning to polka commanded a premium payment in dance schools. In 1847, a dancing academy in the downtown American House Hotel charged a gentleman and a lady a total of six dollars for twelve dance lessons, unless the couple desired instruction in the polka, which involved an unspecified extra payment.

By the 1930s, the city had distinguished itself by creating the "Cleveland-style polka." The dance incorporates an accordion as the dominant instrument and invokes a faster pace than a waltz, although still slower than most other ethnic-style polkas. The origin of the "Cleveland-style polka" can be traced to 1911, when, at the age of twenty, Slovenian-born Matija Arko (later known as Matt Hoyer) settled on East Eighty-Second Street in the Newburgh neighborhood. He constructed, repaired and tuned accordions and founded a musical trio. Believed to be the first artist to record a Slovenian polka (in 1919), Hoyer helped popularize the Cleveland style nationally with his 1927 hit recording "Jaka Na St. Clairu" ("Jack on St. Clair"). Dr. William Lausche, a dentist, pianist, arranger, composer and brother of political icon Frank Lausche, later composed "Cleveland, the Polka Town," featuring the rousing lyrics, "Wedding bells will ring out in Cleveland / That's the place where I intend to settle down / And listen to the rhythm of the polka / In Cleveland, the polka town."

Left: William "Doc" Lausche, an influential figure in developing the "Cleveland-style polka," composed the popular song "Cleveland, the Polka Town." *Courtesy of Cleveland Public Library, Photograph Collection.*

Below: Paul Wilcox hosted the *Polka Varieties* television program for twenty-seven years. In this image, Wilcox chats with polka bandleaders Hank Haller (*left*) and Wally Chips (*right*). *Courtesy of Special Collections, Michael Schwartz Library, Cleveland State University.*

Pioneering radio and television programs expanded Cleveland's polka heritage. Debuting on Cleveland radio in 1929, *The Slovenian Hour* featured polka and waltz music along with community news. The early Cleveland television show *Polka Parade* debuted in 1950. *Polka Varieties*, an hour-long syndicated television program originating in Cleveland, presented prominent national polka bands from 1956 to 1983. Paul Wilcox hosted the show for twenty-seven years even though he never learned how to dance the polka.

Cleveland also produced more than its share of polka bands, from the nationally famous Frankie Yankovic to well-known local groups headed by Lou Trebar, Johnny Pecon, Kenny Bass, the Vadnal brothers (Johnny, Frank and Richie), Eddie Habat, Joey Miskulin, Frankie Mullec and others.

Born in Slovenia, Andy Yankovic immigrated to West Virginia in 1903 and worked as a blacksmith attending mules utilized in coal mines. Coincidently, Rose Mele emigrated from Slovenia to West Virginia that same year and met Andy. The two married in 1910.

In 1915, after authorities accused Andy of bootlegging, he relocated to Cleveland's Collinwood neighborhood with his wife, three daughters and a five-month-old son named Frankie. Following a stint as a crane operator, Andy opened a hardware store near East 160th Street and St. Clair Avenue.

To generate extra income, Andy and Rose rented portions of their home to Slovenian bachelors. Max Zelodec, one of these borders, entertained the household and neighbors by playing the button box. At the age of nine, Frankie observed that Max could become the center of attention anytime he desired. He asked Max to give him lessons, and Frankie quickly learned to play the button box. Although Andy appreciated his son's musical talent, he became dismayed when Frankie switched from a button box to an accordion, explaining to Frankie, "all accordion players are bums."

In the 1930s, while developing his musical career, Frankie worked as a bakery-truck driver and as a pattern maker at the West Steel Casting Company. Lacking a recording contract, he cut his first records at his own expense. Yankovic enhanced his reputation by playing at dances, nightclubs and weddings. During World War II, he earned a Purple Heart fighting in the Battle of the Bulge. In addition to suffering a wound, he endured extensive frostbite. Doctors recommended amputating his frozen fingers, but Yankovic refused.

Following the war, Yankovic emerged as a national star. In 1948, he recorded "Just Because," a 1929 country song, but only after he agreed to purchase the first ten thousand copies. The recording soared onto *Billboard's*

Frankie Yankovic entertained Clevelanders for three decades with polka tours. *Courtesy of the Plain Dealer.*

top-ten hit list. Elvis Presley later covered the song for his 1956 debut album; Paul McCartney and Al Hirt also recorded the Yankovic hit. The next year, Frankie struck gold again with the "Blue Skirt Waltz." Capitalizing on his popularity, Frankie and the band traveled seventy thousand miles annually, mostly by automobile, to perform about three hundred concerts per year from Euclid Beach to Waikiki Beach. The bookings included month-long engagements in Reno and Lake Tahoe.

In 1956, a Yankovic television show (later renamed *Polka Varieties*) debuted while the Fisher Foods grocery chain marketed six volumes of his music on twelve-inch, hi-fi, long-playing albums that sold for ninety-nine cents each. In the 1960s, Yankovic fronted thirty-day polka tours extending from Slovenia into Germany, Austria, Italy and France. Continuing into the 1970s and 1980s, his tours traveled to Hawaii, Mexico City, Acapulco and the Caribbean.

In 1986, Yankovic received the first-ever Grammy Award in the Best Polka Recording category for his album *Seventy Years of Hits.*

The city honored Frankie Yankovic by naming a lot bordering a major intersection in Collinwood "Frankie Yankovic Square." *Courtesy of the author.*

In 1995, the seventy-nine-year-old Yankovic suffered a mild heart attack that caused him to fall from a ladder while attempting to retrieve a piece of band equipment from a crawl space in his garage. Still active two years later, he appeared in Bill Clinton's 1997 Inauguration Day Parade. But his heart condition worsened, and he died of heart failure in 1998. His funeral took place at St. Mary Church on Holmes Avenue. Relatives, friends, polka lovers, politicians and reporters from *Time* and *People* magazines attended the service. He is buried in Calvary Cemetery. To honor Cleveland's polka king, a grassy lot at the intersection of East 152nd Street and Waterloo Road has been named Frankie Yankovic Square.

Lou Trebar, a lifelong Cleveland resident, grew up in the St. Clair neighborhood. At the age of thirteen, he began his sixty-year performing and arranging career. In his teen years, he adapted Johann Strauss waltzes for the accordion and formed his own band while attending East Technical High School. He integrated American jazz into traditional Slovenian music and later added drums, bass and a rhythm guitar to craft a "big band" feel into his polka music. Often sporting a hat, cigar and modified walrus mustache, Trebar teamed up with Johnny Pecon's band in the late 1940s.

As a five-year-old, Johnny Pecon began playing the accordion. Following his graduation from Collinwood High School and service in World War II, he joined the Frankie Yankovic band. Pecon and Yankovic both played the accordion, creating an innovative musical sound at the time. Pecon supplied the accordion accompaniments for Yankovic's hits "Blue Skirt Waltz" and "Just Because." Remaining with Yankovic would have required extensive out-of-town touring. Not wishing to abandon his "day" jobs (first as a gardener with the parks department and later as head custodian at city hall), Pecon left the Yankovic band.

In 1949, Pecon and Lou Trebar founded a band that concentrated on the northeast Ohio polka scene. The duo performed at virtually every local venue noted for polka music. In 1962, patrons of Paderewski's Restaurant on Harvard Avenue enjoyed Pecon's music while consuming sirloin steak, chicken paprikash, tenderloin tips or stuffed cabbage dinners, all priced at $2.95. Pecon also performed at the Broadview Movie Theater on Pearl Road, on the *Goodtime* cruise ship and during period breaks in Cleveland Barons hockey games at the old Cleveland Arena. He used his vacation time from work to win an Arthur Godfrey Talent Scout program and tour Yugoslavia and Hawaii with his band.

Pecon appeared extensively on radio and television polka programs. His own *Polka Time* television show, debuting in 1950, featured three couples

In 1952, the Johnny Pecon band used this postcard to promote their music. *Courtesy of Special Collections, Michael Schwartz Library, Cleveland State University.*

competing in a polka dance contest. Possibly Pecon's most unique polka-playing setting took place on the *TV Auction Party* program. In 1952, Al Wish sold appliances (refrigerators, stoves, washers, dryers, sewing machines, radios, televisions and lamps) in his Appliance Ranch on Turney Road in Maple Heights. On Sundays, customers could purchase a product outright at the labeled price or request an auction in which other potential buyers in the store would participate. The highest bidder received the appliance.

In 1957, Wish created his *TV Auction Party*, with Johnny Pecon providing the musical interludes. The studio audience, during breaks between dancing to polka music, bid on the store's appliances. The prices established on the television program would remain in force for the following week at the Appliance Ranch. Wish and Pecon continued the novel television programming into 1963.

In 1975, more than three thousand polka devotees packed the Euclid Slovenian Home to participate in a twenty-six band tribute honoring Johnny Pecon. Undergoing cancer treatment, the sixty-year-old Pecon could not attend the festivities; he died later that year.

Promoted in 1948 as America's first daily polka show, Kenny Bass's fifteen-minute radio program featured the period's most popular polka recordings. Although the time slot changed to Saturday evenings and then to Sunday mornings, Bass continued playing polka records on radio until the day he died. A Collinwood native, he also launched an early television show and fronted his popular band, Kenny Bass and his Polka Poppers.

In the 1950s, when Bass toured the heavily Slovenian-populated town of Canonsburg, Pennsylvania, a young Bobby Vinton would often stand near the stage in the hope of being asked to perform. Vinton received his chance and developed into a major star with four number-one songs, "Roses Are Red," "Blue Velvet," "There! I've Said It Again" and "Mr. Lonely," along with twenty-seven other chart hits.

During his career, Bass recorded seventeen polka albums and two hundred single recordings, including his own composition, "Lake Erie Polka." The group even appeared in the 1964 movie *One Potato, Two Potato* as the band playing in a wedding scene. Bass also worked in his father's furnace and roofing business. In 1987, following the taping of his weekly radio show, he suffered a cerebral hemorrhage and died.

Johnny Vadnal launched a radio program in 1948 featuring local and coast-to-coast broadcasts from the Bowl Ballroom on East Ninety-Third Street. *Polka Parade*, his early television program, debuted in 1950; Vadnal continued his television show into the mid-1960s. His extensive touring

Left: Johnny Pecon and merchant Al Wish teamed up to create the novel *TV Auction Party*, seen on local television for more than five years. *Courtesy of the* Plain Dealer.

Right: In 1949, Johnny Vadnal and Chester Budny provided the entertainment as the Bowl Ballroom welcomed in the new year. *Courtesy of the* Plain Dealer.

included trips to Europe, Canada and across the United States. His single and album recordings remained popular through five decades; Vadnal is especially noted for "Yes Dear Waltz," "Two-timing You," "Good Time Polka" and the "No Beer on Sunday" polka.

The continuity of the Vadnal band is vividly illustrated by the career of Frank D. Mahnic Sr. Born in Slovenia, two-year-old Mahnic and his parents immigrated to Cleveland in 1924. He joined the Vadnal band at the age of seventeen, remaining as a singer and saxophonist for nearly fifty-two years until just prior to his death.

In 1996, at the age of seventy-four, Johnny Vadnal retired when arthritis hampered his accordion playing. His professional finale took place at the Slovenian Workman's Home in Collinwood, on the very same stage where he began his career as a teenager some fifty-nine years earlier.

Frank Vadnal, a graduate of Collinwood High School, joined his sister Valeria and brothers Johnny and Tony to form the Vadnal Quartet. The group performed at Collinwood's Slovenian Workman's Home, created a radio program in the 1950s, appeared on local polka television programs and toured extensively in Ohio, Michigan and Illinois. Frankie, who also worked at Addressograph-Multigraph, died while performing in a Pennsylvania polka festival.

Richie Vadnal began his accordion playing at the age of four and organized his own band as a teenager. Richie also toured with Frankie Yankovic and performed with the Three Suns. In 1966, he took over the Johnny Vadnal Orchestra and hosted tours to Slovenia, Hawaii, the Caribbean and throughout the United States.

Born in Cleveland in 1926, Eddie Habat started playing the accordion at age seven. Four years later, he launched his career playing at parties and weddings. In 1942, when he had reached the age of sixteen, Eddie led the Johnny Pecon Orchestra while Pecon served in the navy. Eddie later fronted his own orchestra and recorded for Decca.

At the age of thirteen, Joey Miskulin played accordion with the Frankie Yankovic band. By the 1970s, Miskulin acted as an arranger, studio musician and producer. He arranged the Grammy Award–winning Frankie Yankovic album *Seventy Years of Hits*. He later hosted his *Polka Time USA* television program. In 1987, Miskulin relocated to Nashville and developed a new career as Joey, the Cowpolka King.

Frankie Mullec's immigrant parents owned a grocery store on Waterloo Road in Collinwood. As a teenager, Mullec played his accordion at local taverns. By the late 1940s, he had established a popular polka band with a national reputation. The band toured the Midwest and recorded "Tell Me a Story," a hit song across the country. His recording company suggested the band incorporate a female singer. The person Mullec hired became his wife of nearly sixty years. The family transformed the old grocery store into Mullec's Lounge Bar, where he played for fifteen years. He later entertained at Yankovic's Steakhouse and the Slovene Home for the Aged on Neff Road.

Following the Vatican II initiative in the mid-1960s, the Catholic Church allowed masses to incorporate customs reflecting different cultures and languages. For most Catholics in northeast Ohio, this change involved a conversion from Latin to English (or a different language in strongly concentrated ethnic areas). In 1971, Youngstown's Reverend George Balasko created the "polka mass," a worship service integrating polka tunes into a traditional mass. A polka enthusiast himself, Balasko even played the

POL-KATS PRESENT THEIR Turkey Hop

5 — Bands — 5

Continuous Music
and Dancing from
8 'til 1:00

WED., NOV. 22

Slovenian Nat'l Home
E. 80th, off Union

In 1961, the Newburgh Slovenian National Hall booked five polka bands for a Wednesday evening "Turkey Hop" the day before Thanksgiving. *Courtesy of the* Plain Dealer.

banjo in a polka band at St. Mary's Seminary in Norwood, Ohio. During a visit to Slovenia, Balasko attended a Catholic mass in which parishioners sang a hymn to the tune of "When the Saints Go Marching In." This experience provided the inspiration for his unique "polka mass" concept. While the words are consistent with conventional Catholic services, a polka rhythm is incorporated into the music as, for example, the congregation prepares for Communion by singing *The Lord's Prayer* to the tune of "Blue Skirt Waltz."

Turkeys, pumpkin pies and polka music have combined to create a longstanding Cleveland Thanksgiving tradition that began in the late 1940s. In 1948, Johnny Vadnal staged a Thanksgiving polka dance at the Bowl Ballroom. A year later, Vadnal provided the music for an annual Thanksgiving eve dance sponsored by the Benedictine High School Alumni Association. In 1961, on the day before Thanksgiving, the Slovenian National Home in Newburgh presented five polka bands participating in a "Turkey Hop." The next year, the Aragon Ballroom on West Twenty-Fifth Street organized a "Polka Jamboree" with three bands performing on the Wednesday before Thanksgiving.

These events comprised a mere warmup for what would become one of the nation's most spectacular Thanksgiving polka events. In 1964, Slovenian radio personality Tony Petkovsek began a still-thriving Thanksgiving Slovenian Festival and Dance that has grown from a local event into a national phenomenon, sometimes even attracting international performers and enthusiasts.

A second-generation Slovenian American born in 1941, Petkovsek spent his early years living above his parents' tavern (the Birch Bar) in the St. Clair neighborhood. In 1961, while working at his parents' bar, Petkovsek originated a half-hour radio polka show. He performed disc jockey duties, spinning the best of the classic and new Slovenian polka offerings. The show continued for decades, with Petkovsek occasionally changing the air times and radio stations.

In 1977, when WXEN switched from an ethnic format to rock music, Petkovsek found himself temporarily out of a job. The Slovenian community immediately protested the change. Ralph Perk, Cleveland's ethnic mayor, considered the WXEN move a civic outrage and organized a mass demonstration at the downtown Music Hall. Two thousand avid polka fans showed up in zero-degree weather to express their disapproval. Petkovsek attended the demonstration and suggested that Slovenians purchase their own radio station. Attendees immediately offered pledges to finance his idea, including one for $2,000. Petkovsek quickly found a new station for his polka music and a new broadcasting venue—Tony's Polka Village on East 185th Street, a record store that he owned. In 2012, after broadcasting radio shows for fifty years, Petkovsek cut back to only a Saturday afternoon show.

Meanwhile, Petkovsek's Thanksgiving Slovenian Festival and Dance became an immediate success. Within a few years of its inception, the Thanksgiving party attracted polka devotees in vans, buses and planes from Pennsylvania, Illinois, Wisconsin, Indiana, Minnesota, Iowa, California, Alaska, Missouri and Florida to the St. Clair Avenue Slovenian National Home. By the late 1970s, simultaneous entertainment had expanded into three separate halls within the St. Clair Avenue venue. In 1978, the festival presented the premiere performance of the thirty-five-piece United Slovenian Society Band.

In 1975, Jeff Pecon, Frankie Yankovic and many other polka bands combined to present ten hours of continuous music at Cleveland's huge Municipal Stadium. *Courtesy of the Plain Dealer.*

In 1982, the festival moved to St. Joseph High School on East 185th Street, where it consumed two floors of the school's auditorium and expanded to provide polka music through the entire Thanksgiving weekend. In 1990 and 1991, the festival expanded into a three-day event in the Grand Ballroom of the downtown Stouffer Tower City Plaza Hotel. In 1992, the holiday polka party relocated to the downtown Marriott Hotel, where it continues to the present day. A bakery worker residing in Holland used most of his life savings to travel across the Atlantic Ocean to attend the 1998 party because he enjoyed polka music. George

Voinovich never missed a Thanksgiving party as Cleveland mayor, Ohio governor or U.S. senator.

New generations of Slovenian polka performers continue to enhance the Cleveland-style polka legacy. By the mid-1970s, Jeff Pecon (the son of Johnny Pecon) had established himself as a first-rate polka performer. He enhanced his reputation in the 1980s by headlining polka cruise parties from Cleveland to the Caribbean and polka automobile trips to Atlantic City, Niagara Falls and Ontario.

In his formative years, Joey Tomsick started accordion lessons and sang in a Slovenian youth chorus. While a student at John Carroll University in the mid-1980s, he founded a polka band. As a college sophomore, he and the band toured California for ten days during a break in classes. Tomsick's 1986 album *Proud of Cleveland* includes his own compositions "Tower City Waltz," "Collinwood Polka" and "Lakeside Waltz."

Born in Collinwood in 1967, Bob Kravos, a great nephew of Frankie Yankovic, received mentoring by Yankovic and Joey Miskulin. Following his graduation from high school, Kravos toured with Yankovic, providing opening entertainment for Bob Hope, Marie Osmond and other stars. In 1987, Kravos formed his own band and continues to perform in northeast Ohio.

The Cleveland-style polka is approaching the anniversary of its first century. The legacy is kept alive with performers such as Pecon, Tomsick and Kravos, the annual downtown Thanksgiving polka party weekend and the Slovenian National Homes.

15

Slovenian Sports

Slammers, Slingers and Sluggers

Demonstrating a passion for sports, the St. Clair Avenue Slovenian neighborhood produced a pair of nationally known boxers, a noted wrestler and a major league baseball star. Meanwhile, a Pro Bowl member of the Cleveland Browns grew up in Collinwood.

In 1923, eighteen-year-old Frankie (Simoncic) Simms (the "Slam-Bang Slovenian") emerged as a promising young heavyweight boxer. Three years later, after dominating the local amateur scene, the broad-shouldered Simms turned professional. His fast and powerful right hand generated a string of early knockouts that placed Frankie on a seeming fast track to stardom.

Early in his professional career, Frankie developed an odd identity predicament. Hired as a substitute boxer in Jackson, Michigan, he replaced "K.O." Billy Clemmons, who failed to show up for a fight. Not expecting that Frankie would create any excitement, the promoters never bothered to announce the substitution. Following Frankie's surprise knockout victory, Jackson boxing fans demanded to see more of the fighter they knew as "K.O." Clemmons. Frankie Simms returned using the Clemmons name and knocked out ten more opponents. Meanwhile, the real Billy Clemmons continued his boxing career, although not in Jackson. Bookies familiar with the situation speculated on how to handle the betting confusion if the two fighters ever battled each other.

On July 3, 1931, Frankie knocked out Boston's Joe Vincha in the first round of a preliminary fight leading up to the Max Schmeling/Young Stribling match that opened the brand-new Cleveland Municipal Stadium.

In the early 1930s, Frankie's major strength continued to be his devastating knockout punch. Unfortunately, he never developed the finesse to avoid absorbing the equally punishing hits delivered by his opponents. Frankie's declining career developed into a series of knockouts, either for himself or his adversaries. In 1934, a Canadian light-heavyweight champion knocked Frankie down for two nine-counts in the first round. Frankie hit the canvas four more times in the second round, enough falls to end the fight. Frankie continued to box until 1939. A quarter of a century later, he was working as a taxicab driver in Shreveport, Louisiana, where he died at the age of sixty.

In 1927, experts ranked seventeen-year-old Eddie Simms (the "Slugging Slovenian") as the best amateur heavyweight fighter in Ohio. Three years later, the success of his older brother Frankie inspired Eddie to turn professional. He knocked out his first opponent in ninety seconds in the first round. Beginning in October 1932, Eddie ran up a streak of thirteen consecutive wins, more than enough to attract national attention.

Hard-punching Frankie Simms emerged from the St. Clair neighborhood to sustain a sixteen-year boxing career. *Courtesy of Cleveland Public Library, Photograph Collection.*

After a dreadful trouncing at Public Hall in 1934, Eddie's manager demanded that the fighter choose between a career in boxing or playing the accordion. Eddie picked the music option. At one point, both Frankie and Eddie Simms combined with local polka legend Matt Hoyer to form the Hoyer Trio. Four months following his career-altering decision, Eddie returned to the ring.

In 1935, Eddie fought the reigning heavyweight champion, Max Baer, in a four-round unofficial bout at Public Hall. Baer got the better of Eddie, but he severely battered both of his hands in conquering Simms. When Baer retired, he named Eddie as the hardest puncher he had ever faced.

On December 14, 1936, Eddie gained a chance to reach the big-time boxing stratum by fighting Joe Louis, another rapidly rising star, in Cleveland's Public Hall. Not even his closest friends thought Eddie could beat Louis. According to Robert Dolgan, a *Plain Dealer* sportswriter and fellow Slovenian, Eddie trained for the match primarily by playing his accordion and feasting on wine, women and song.

Eddie landed three quick punches that, after the fight, Louis claimed he did not remember: "It didn't feel as if Simms hit me at all. Maybe he did, but I didn't feel anything." But twenty-one seconds into the bout, it really didn't matter what Eddie had accomplished. Louis hit him with a hard left hook, his first and only punch of the match, knocking the Slovenian to the canvas. Eddie staggered to his feet after an eight-count. After assuring the referee that he felt fine, Eddie invited the referee to take a walk with him, suggesting the roof of the building. The contest ended when Eddie informed the referee that he could not see clearly, if at all.

Plain Dealer reporter John Dietrich commented, "He couldn't have dropped quicker if someone had climbed up the ring side and popped him with a blackjack." A sarcastic Tommy Tucker, covering the fight for the *Cleveland News*, didn't seem to understand why Joe Louis impressed everyone: "The way that Louis wasted time makes you wonder how he ever expects to get anywhere." Tucker continued his commentary by noting that Louis had only hit Eddie with one punch in the entire fight.

Eddie presented his own recollection of the match: "I can't understand what happened. I never saw the punch coming. I must have walked into it. It didn't hurt. It just put out the lights." But he viewed his loss very philosophically: "It was an easy $4,000." Eddie had a valid point; adjusted for inflation, his time in the ring would today amount to earning more than $8,000,000 an hour.

Following the Joe Louis debacle, the Slugging Slovenian continued his fight career, but he retired after losing seven of his last eight fights. By the late 1930s, Eddie had formed an orchestra that performed at the Twilight Ballroom on St. Clair Avenue and other local spots. During World War II, Eddie served in the navy, where he temporarily revived his boxing career. In addition, he appeared as a boxer in the Ann Sothern film *Ringside Maisie* and in the Spencer Tracy and Katharine Hepburn movie *Woman of the Year*. After the war, Eddie relocated to the Los Angeles area, where he took on mostly uncredited boxing roles in films, including *The Right Cross* (William Powell), *Iron Man* (Jeff Chandler) and *Sailor Beware* (Dean Martin and Jerry Lewis). He worked as a nightclub bouncer and, for twenty years, as a steamfitter. Retired, Eddie moved to Las Vegas in 1989 and died in 1995 at the age of eighty-five.

Prior to embarking on a wrestling career, Ferdinand "Fred" Bozic finished as a runner-up in Cleveland's 1932 Golden Gloves heavyweight

Baseball all-star Al Milnar registered many wins for the Cleveland Indians. *Courtesy of Cleveland Public Library, Photograph Collection.*

boxing finals. As a 220-pound wrestler, Clevelanders knew him as the "Slovenian Slammer" and "Fearless Fred." But his opponents created a less flattering set of names for Bozic. Referees often disqualified the "Rassling Rogue" because of his nasty behavior in the ring, which included hitting and kicking his opponents far below the belt. A well-known grappler at the Central Armory, Cleveland Arena, Municipal Stadium and other local venues, Bozic at times required police to intervene because of the mayhem he created in the ring. He fought about 250 matches prior to retiring to a job as a pipefitter for the City of Cleveland. In 1980, he died from a heart attack at the age of seventy.

The St. Clair neighborhood labeled southpaw pitcher Albert Joseph Milnar the "Slick Slovenian Slinger." Signed by the Cleveland Indians to a minor-league contract, Milnar joined the club's Zanesville farm team. In a 1933 exhibition game against the big leaguers, Milnar struck out eighteen Indians on the way to hurling a three-hitter. Two years later in New Orleans, he won seventeen consecutive games. Milnar made his major-league debut in 1938. In 1940, he won eighteen games against ten losses. In the American League, only Cleveland's Bob Feller and Detroit's Bobo Newsom won more games that year. His four shutouts tied future hall of famers Feller and Chicago's Ted Lyons for the major-league best. As an American League all-star, Milnar earned about $9,000 per year.

In 1941, Milnar signed for a $14,000 base pay plus a bonus for every win over fifteen. The next year, he missed a no-hitter against Detroit by giving up his first hit with two outs in the ninth inning. With the score tied at zero, Milnar pitched fourteen innings, giving up only one other hit. Suspended because of darkness, the Tigers won the game when it resumed the next day. Milnar's career ended in 1946. He died in Cleveland in 2005 at the age of ninety-one.

Born in Fairmont, West Virginia, in 1924 to Slovenian immigrants, Tony Adamle grew up in Collinwood. Following a stellar football career at Collinwood High School, Paul Brown recruited Adamle to play for Ohio State University. He attended Ohio State only briefly before leaving for military service, where he became a radio operator on air force bombing missions. After the war, he returned to Ohio State for one year but then joined Paul Brown, now the coach of the Cleveland Browns. Adamle, a linebacker and running back, played a total of six seasons with the Browns (1947–51 and 1954) and appeared in a championship game every year; the Browns won five of the six contests.

In 1947, Brown doubled Adamle's salary for one game when the linebacker made four tackles on the goal line during a game at Yankee Stadium. Adamle participated in the first two Pro Bowl games following the 1950 and 1951 seasons. He also played in the now-defunct College All-Star Game (in which the NFL champion competed against a team composed of college all-stars). When Paul Brown criticized the defense following the Cleveland Browns' 1951 title game loss, an irritated Adamle retired from football and enrolled in medical school. While in school, the Chicago Cardinals hired him to scout other NFL teams on a part-time basis.

Adamle agreed to return to the Browns in 1954 to replace an injured player. To ensure that his medical studies would not be hampered, he insisted on practicing only one day a week. Amazingly, just a few days after he scouted the Browns team for the Chicago Cardinals, Adamle donned a Browns uniform to compete against the Cardinals.

Following his second retirement, Adamle earned a medical degree from Western Reserve University, established a medical practice in Kent, Ohio, and played in a polka band. His son Mike played professional football and, following an injury-related retirement, became a well-known sports commentator.

Slovenian Robert Perry Golic (better known as Bob) grew up in the St. Clair neighborhood. After winning the Ohio heavyweight high school wrestling championship by defeating future Olympic participant Harold Smith, Golic earned All-American football and wrestling honors at Notre Dame prior to a fourteen-year career in the NFL that included seven years with the Cleveland Browns. Mike Golic, Bob's younger brother and also a Notre Dame graduate, played in the National Football League for eight years before co-hosting the ESPN morning program *Mike & Mike*. The father of Bob and Mike had completed a seven-year career in the Canadian Football League.

A women's athletic club poses for a 1913 photograph with their male coach. *Courtesy of Beth Piwkowski.*

In addition to sports stars, countless other sports-minded Slovenians throughout Cleveland took part in a wide variety of sporting activities. Young boys socked a rubber ball around an elementary school yard on Addison Road. Virtually everything not caught by the opposing team resulted in a single. But a ball that bounced off the school's roof and not snared by the opponent counted as a home run.

Bocce, a game played in the days of Julius Caesar and renamed *balina* in parts of Yugoslavia, resembles outdoor bowling. Played on courts ranging from clay to grass (and sometimes on indoor courts), the game's objective is to roll a larger ball as close as possible to an already-in-place smaller ball. Veterans of the St. Clair neighborhood still consider Frank Lausche one of the area's best balina players.

Early in the twentieth century, Slovenians organized baseball teams and even leagues. Just prior to World War I, amateur baseball championship matches at Brookside Park drew as many as 100,000 spectators. The teams' lineups often consisted of immigrants and first-generation Americans with eastern European backgrounds. Relatives and fans cheered the players in a colorful array of native languages. During the Great Depression, the Slovenian Lassies participated in a female industrial softball league; Slovenian females also organized a ping-pong team.

Slovenian bowling leagues had flourished even prior to World War I and continued in the Great Depression. In 1930, seventeen Slovenian bowling teams entered a Public Hall tournament. Responding to the popularity of bowling, Slovenian National Homes installed alleys in their facilities. Some of them continue to host bowling leagues.

The Maple Lanes and Tavern, a still-existing bowling alley and bar on St. Clair Avenue, debuted in the 1920s. In the 1960s, a pair of husband-and-wife couples, Gwyn and Josephine "Chickie" Reeves and Ed and Ann "Butchie" Abranovich, purchased the facility. Sisters Chickie and Butchie grew up in the St. Clair neighborhood, the daughters of Slovenian immigrants; Gwyn and Chickie even lived above the bowling alley. Sons, daughters and cousins of the families learned to set pins. Maple Lanes pinsetters included cousins Gwyn Reeves Jr. and Mark Abranovich, along with Kate Rogers, an eighth-grade cousin of Mark. When Chickie died, at her request, she was buried wearing her bowling shoes.

In 1964, Viado "Wally" Pisorn emigrated from Slovenia with his parents and nine siblings (five sisters and four brothers). He purchased the Harbor Inn, a bar in Cleveland's Flats district with a long history of serving factory workers, sailors, lawyers, judges and celebrities, including Bob Hope, Jack

The site of the Maple Lanes has been a bowling alley and tavern for nearly a century. *Courtesy of the author.*

Lemmon and Robert De Niro. While not normally a Slovenian hangout, on June 18, 2010, the Harbor Inn turned into a prominent, if temporary, Slovenian haunt. Inspired by Slovenia's spirited performances in the World Cup soccer tournament, Wally tuned in his televisions to the match between Slovenia and the United States. Strolling accordionists entertained Slovenian patrons who joined in to sing old folk songs and dance polkas before and after the contest, which ended in a 2–2 tie.

Slovenian Nut Potica Recipe

Dough Ingredients

2 cakes compressed yeast
½ cup lukewarm milk
1 tablespoon sugar
6½ to 7 cups sifted all-purpose flour
¾ cup sugar
1 teaspoon salt
1 cup scalded and slightly cooled milk
4 beaten egg yolks
2 beaten whole eggs
½ cup softened sweet butter

Dough Instructions

Crumble yeast into lukewarm milk. Add 1 tablespoon sugar. Stir and set aside until foamy.

Sift flour, sugar and salt into a large bowl; make a well in the center. Add cooled scalded milk, beaten egg yolks, eggs, butter and yeast. Mix thoroughly with wooden spoon.

Knead with your hands for about ten minutes until the dough is no longer sticky. The kneading can be done in a bowl or on a floured cloth.

Form into soft ball and place in a greased bowl. Cover with wax paper and a damp cloth and allow the mixture to rise in a warm place for about 1½ hours, until the dough is doubled.

Filling Ingredients

½ pint sweet cream
½ cup butter
½ cup honey
2 pounds ground walnuts
1 tablespoon grated lemon peel
1 teaspoon vanilla
1 teaspoon salt
2 egg yolks
½ pint sour cream
2 stiffly beaten egg whites
1¾ cups sugar
½ pound golden raisins

Filling Instructions

Scald sweet cream, butter and honey together and pour over the ground nuts. Add a lemon peel, vanilla and salt and mix together. Fold in egg yolks, sour cream and stiffly beaten egg whites.

Add more egg whites if mixture is too dry.

Blend in sugar and set aside.

Preparation

Punch down risen dough and place on floured cloth spread on a table. Use a rolling pin to roll to about ¼-inch thickness (about 36 inches long and 22 inches wide). Spread nut filling on top of dough evenly, leaving about 4 inches of plain dough on one end. Sprinkle top of nut filling with raisins and add a generous sprinkling of sugar to the top of the raisins.

Lift the long side of the dough with cloth and coax to roll as a jelly roll. After dough is completely rolled, cut with a floured spatula into four 9-inch pieces; pinch seam of dough closed.

Place, seam side down, into four greased 9-by-5-by-3-inch bread pans. Prick dough with toothpicks on top to prevent bubble. Cover with cloth and allow to rise for forty-five minutes.

Brush tops with melted butter.

Baking

Bake in an oven preheated to 325 degrees for forty-five minutes to one hour or until an inserted toothpick comes out clean. Let stand in pans ten to fifteen minutes after removing from oven. Then remove to cooling racks to cool completely.

Each roll makes twelve to fourteen slices.

Bibliography

Alexander, June Granatir. *Daily Life in Immigrant America (1870–1920)*. Westport, CT: Greenwood Press, 2007.

Bonutti, Karl, and George Prpic. *Selected Ethnic Communities of Cleveland: A Socio-Economic Study.* Cleveland, OH: Cleveland State University, 1974.

Corsellis, John, and Marcus Ferrar. *Slovenia 1945*. London: I.B. Tauris, 2010.

Jozwiak, Kathleen L. *Cleveland-Style Polka Directory, A Snapshot*. Willoughby, OH: St. Monica, 1998.

Klemencic, Matjaz. *Slovenes of Cleveland*. Novo Mesto, Slovenia: Dolenjska Zalozba, 1995.

Ledbetter, Eleanor E. *The Jugoslavs of Cleveland*. Cleveland, OH: Cleveland Americanization Committee, 1918.

Milac, Metod M. *Resistance, Imprisonment, & Forced Labor: A Slovene Student in World War II*. New York: Peter Lang, 2002.

Oman, Monsignor John J. *Fifty Years: Saint Lawrence (1901–1951)*. Cleveland, OH: Saint Lawrence Church, 1951.

Pap, Michael S. *Ethnic Communities of Cleveland*. University Heights, OH: John Carroll University, 1973.

Rebol, Rev. Anthony. *History of St. Mary of the Assumption Church and School*. Cleveland, OH, 1962.

Schneider, Russell. *The Cleveland Indians Encyclopedia*. Philadelphia, PA: Temple University Press, 1996.

St. Vitus Church. *St. Vitus Church (1893–1993)*. Cleveland, OH, 1993.

Wittke, Carl. *We Who Built America*. Cleveland, OH: Western Reserve University, 1964.

Index

About the Author

Since native Clevelander Alan Dutka's retirement from a business career, he has published six Cleveland history books: *Historic Movie Theaters of Downtown Cleveland*; *Misfortune on Cleveland's Millionaires' Row*; *AsiaTown Cleveland: From Tong Wars to Dim Sum*; *Cleveland Calamities: A History of Storm, Fire and Pestilence*; *East Fourth Street: The Rise, Decline, and Rebirth of an Urban Cleveland Street* and *Cleveland's Short Vincent: The Theatrical Grill and Its Notorious Neighbors*. During his business career, he authored four marketing research books, including *Customer Satisfaction Research*, a primary selection of the Newbridge Executive Book Club that has been translated into Spanish and Japanese. Dutka is a popular speaker at historical societies, libraries, community centers and the Music Box Supper Club. He has appeared on the *Feagler & Friends*, *Applause* and *7 Minutes with Russ Mitchell* television programs, along with radio programs, including Dee Perry's *Around Noon* and Jacqueline Gerber's morning program. He has been interviewed by PBS, the *Lorain Morning Journal* and France 24 Television.